In That Land:
A Seedtime and Harvest Approach
to Finding A Wife

Dale E Lott, Jr.

978-0-615-33996-2

Published in Atlanta, Ga by 1978 Press

Cover Design by Divine Image Graphics
Cover Photo by Helmuth Boeger
Editing and layout by Suzanne Hocking

Acknowledgments

This book has been a long time coming and I'd like to thank everyone involved with the process of bringing this into fruition.

Of course, the first people who come to mind are my parents. They are the reason I am here in the first place with all of their love and impartation. However, I do have another set of parents I must thank as well – my pastors, Creflo and Taffi Dollar. They have fed me well with the Word. To these four people I owe undying devotion. Before I move on there are a few other people I must acknowledge as well.

Ministers Michael Tyler Smith and Michael Orion Carter – Thank you for seeing me during periods of my life when I felt like I was on the back side of the desert.

Kelly Cole and Andre Dennis – Thank you for stoking the fire and connecting me with people I would not have met on my own. Kelly, I told you, "I'm coming."

Tamiko Harris – You've been the best friend I could have. Thanks for helping me with the initial edit and review of my book. You're honesty brought much needed change.

Damon Danielson – Thank you for being 'the man from a far country....' Your design is truly amazing. God knew who was right for the job.

Helmuth Boeger – Your generosity was more than I expected and your eye as a photographer is astounding.

Autumn and Morgan, my two beautiful girls – You inspire me to be better.

My AMG brethren – Thank you... just because.

Suzanne Hocking – You're the greatest. Your work has been superb. Thanks for being so patient with me. Cheers!

TO MY WIFE

My lifelong pursuit of you has led me to my destiny – fulfilling God's purpose for my life. This is as much a testament to you as it is my willingness to follow Christ, because all that God taught me was in preparation for you. May life with me never be a disappointment to you.

Table of Contents

Introduction

I saw her in a dream, but I couldn't see her face, just her hair. When I awoke I knew this wasn't an ordinary dream. Sure, when you're sixteen years old, you dream about a lot of girls. Yet this was different.

All of my life I had been looking for the 'one', which is surprisingly odd for a kid. I never cared about being a player, or sleeping with as many girls as possible. I just wanted mine.

So on a spring day in 1995, after dealing with tremendous depression, insecurity, and a crushing heartbreak, I dreamed a dream. This dream put me on a quest to locate my wife as I went off to college in the fall of 1996, even though I had no idea who I was looking for.

After another heartbreak in the winter months of early 1997, I decided to have a conversation with God, because I could not understand why I seemed to be having a hard time with this, because I'd assumed the dream was a harbinger of an imminent reality. That conversation was life changing.

"Do you want her back?" God asked me.

I remember that question like it was yesterday. It shocked me, because intitially I thought it was a dumb question. However, my response shocked me even more. Before my lips could form the word 'yes', my spirit spoke.

"No, not until I get over this hurt. Because, if I'm not happy unless we're together, then she is my god. And I refuse to have anyone but You determine my happiness."

The angels applauded [okay, maybe I'm exaggerating] as I passed that loyalty test.

God quickly spoke again.

"What do you want? Make a list."

At that moment, I began to jot down a few things. Well, okay, forty seven things. As I compiled this list of my desires, I realized I was not just arbitrarily throwing out shallow wants. I my list was so detailed, because I was trying to capture everything my imagination could see.

Throughout my teenage years, I spent so much time with God that I had strong idea of who I was and the general arena my purpose was to serve. I knew I wasn't average. God had a very specific arena of life in which I was to abide. Therefore, it was easy for me to begin to formulate a picture of my wife according to my purpose and desires. However, I couldn't quite describe it all.

Sensing my frustration or incompleteness, God spoke a simple and often overlooked truth to me that has become both a magnet and a thorn in my side. He said:

"Your wife already exist. She doesn't magically appear the moment you see. But, right now she is living life somewhere. Begin to pray for her like you would pray for a friend."

From that moment forward, I began to pray for my wife, both in english and in tongues (the spirit). That led to such an acute awareness of who my wife is that I've become blinded by that image. Very few women come close. If you've ever been looking for something specific to the point where you just knew it when you saw it then understand my level of selectivity. The bad thing is it really puts a damper on attending a singles' mixer when you can eliminate nincty percent of the room in five minutes.

If we ended there, the story would be great. How amazing. I developed an image, which served as a magnet; leading me to my wife. The end. Unfortunately, I had one huge problem – the impatience of lonliness.

I think of my life in terms of two great men of faith, Abraham and Moses. Before either of these men developed great faith, they had to battle impatience. God gave them promises, yet they couldn't wait on God. Their impatience stemmed primarily out of unbelief. It caused them to try and help God, moving before it was time, adding great hardship to their lives.

From the moment God spoke to me, my impatience stemming from lonliness caused me to enter into several relationships I should not have been involved in; not because I wanted to be loved, but because I wanted to love.

Until I had this encounter with God, I was legendary for being romantic. It did not matter if the female was short or tall, dark or light-skinned, thin or thick, I had not any preconceived notions about what I wanted, so it was easy for me to love almost anybody hard and genuine.

That changed that night. No longer was I able to love just anybody. I would see a young lady and something about her would catch my eye. I was attracted to her. However, I knew she was not my wife. She did not match the image God helped me develop. Instead of walking away, I would pursue, because I wanted to love; to be in love; to have someone to hold; to make someone feel special; to not be alone. I remembered what it felt like to love from the bottom of my heart; sincere and pure.

With those females it was different, though. After the infatuation wore off, I was still empty, so this image God gave me became a thorn in my side. I was now too selective for something not inspired by God that left me empty and unfulfilled anyway. Besides, my gift to write poetry and songs – to be romantic – only flows out of pure love, which means my purpose is being denied when I'm in a wrong relationship.

The more I think about it, the only things those wrong relationships gave me was heartache, despair, and children (two beautiful girls). Only recently did I realize most of my problems stemmed from the fact that they were never designed to fill that particular void in my heart.

I would sit in a room and talk with them, but that wouldn't fill the void in my heart. So, I would hold their hand, then hold them, then kiss them, then have sex with them. Yet, none of it filled that void.

Have I ever seen someone similar to the image God helped me develop?

Yes, but idle relationships hindered the development of that relationship. They gave the wrong impression of me. My only true desire was being overshadowed and blocked by my fear of being alone. God promised I wouldn't lack (Prov 34:9-10), and because

I had placeholders, I didn't lack, though they weren't what I truly desired.

I'm ashamed I let fear stop me, because when I was in the presence of this particular female, I was completely content – no need to try and artificially stimulate intimacy. However, God didn't give up on me. He continued to push me and teach me where I was going wrong and what to do to correct it. He has given me the gameplan; the blueprint. Now He has tasked me to share it with you. Enjoy and grow.

The Compass

"Dale, you need to change your inner conversation."

"Dale, sometimes you give off the impression that you're lazy, but you're not. You're fearful. You have a fearful laziness. You know what you need to do, but you are afraid to step out and do it."

It's funny how God has people impart pieces of wisdom about you that you'd never considered. Those two statements were made to me by two co-workers, Loren Knowles and Walter Holston.

Those statements marked me. I grew up confessing the Word (yes, I practice naming it and claiming it!), but I wasn't getting as much result as people who spent less time with God than I did. This state of affairs frustrated me terribly, because I could not understand why I was unproductive. Those two statements were the beginning of God speaking to me concerning my inner image.

God destined me to be great, but I was living in fear. Here I was, a man empowered by God, yet unable to fully access that power to get results. What was the root cause of my ineffectiveness?

My image of myself.

In Numbers 13, God commanded Moses to send out twelve men to spy out the land He promised to give them. Upon their return, only Caleb and Joshua gave a report indicating they were able to go in and possess the land. The other ten men gave a bad report. While they agreed it was a wonderful place, they did not believe they were capable of taking possession of the land. Listen to their report in their own words.

> And they gave the children of
> Israel a bad report of the land which they had spied
> out, saying, "The land through which we have gone as
> spies is a land that devours its inhabitants, and all the
> people whom we saw in it are men of great stature.
> There we saw the giants (the descendants of Anak
> came from giants); and we were like grasshoppers in
> our own sight, and so were we in their sight."
>
> Num 13:33

Notice that how they saw themselves was the determining factor in whether or not they fulfilled God's will and, ultimately, how people viewed them. So it was with me. My picture of myself was controlling me more than my picture of God. No matter how we view God, if we do not see ourselves as He sees us, then we can not accomplish what He has placed before us. Oftentimes, we do not need more of God; we need more confidence in ourselves, in what He has said about us.

Where does confidence come from?

Confidence comes from the positive inner images we have concerning ourselves or particular activities. It is possible to be confident in one area because we have a positive image of it, yet be insecure in another because of our negative image in that area. Therefore, if we desire to have confidence in the tasks God has assigned for us to accomplish, then we must have a positive inner image. That positive inner image only comes from spending time in God's Word and allowing it to change the image we have of ourselves. If we do not allow our self-image to be changed, then the power of God's Word is severely hampered. The only thing that can hinder the operation of God's Word in our lives is unbelief, or lack of confidence.

Why is this?

To answer this question, let me give you a crash course on the way our minds work. Understanding this process will make it easier to change your inner image through God's Word.

The human mind is actually comprised of two compartments. The first compartment is the conscious mind. There is where you are able to reason, go over information, and make decisions. This is the part of the mind of which you are aware of its functions.

The second compartment is the subconscious mind. At this level, the functions of your mind are autonomic and meta-cognitive, meaning they happen without your direct intervention and without you being aware of the occurrence. You don't have to tell your heart to beat, or your lungs to breathe, or your liver to cleanse your system – all of these functions are controlled subconsciously. These functions have been imprinted on your subconscious mind, and whatever is imprinted on the subconscious mind is automatically executed. The subconscious mind literally controls your life. Therefore, it is often referred to as the creator of your life as Prov 4:23 tells us:

Guard your heart
[subconscious mind] with all diligence for out of it
spring the issues [forces, situations, conditions] of life.

Your life flows out of you, because the conscious and subconscious compartments of your mind work together to create your life's circumstances. The conscious mind allows you to filter the thoughts, images, and words you receive from internal and external sources. It is the gatekeeper to the subconscious mind.

Whatever your conscious mind continually sees, imagines, thinks, hears, and says will eventually be accepted as true and become imbedded in your subconscious mind. Once your subconscious mind accepts something as true, it automatically executes and brings it to pass in your life.

The thoughts and beliefs you feed your subconscious mind create images that become the blueprint for your life. Your subconscious is tasked with the responsibility of producing the blueprints given to it.

Have you ever met someone who believed they would never find a good man or woman? Did you notice they never did? Why was this so? Because their mind's belief ensured that their physical life lined up with the image imprinted on their subconscious mind.

Your subconscious mind never intends to bring you any harm; it is merely carrying out what has been deposited into it. Your conscious mind is the farmer and your subconscious mind is the garden. The subconscious doesn't argue with the conscious mind; it doesn't reason; it doesn't understand jokes; it doesn't recognize sarcasm, and it doesn't translate figures of speech. It merely brings into existence what is deposited into it.

Every condition in your life grew out of the thoughts, images, and words imprinted on your subconscious mind. You are what you think, imagine, see, hear, say and do all day long. This is why I could not produce results. I was saying good things, but my thoughts and inner image were negative. My negativity outweighed and cancelled out my positivity. Therefore, negativity was imprinted on my subconscious mind (after all, I gave it so much attention) where it reproduced. Consequently, I had no confidence because I did not fully see myself the way God saw me.

However, once I understood how my mind worked, I defeated depression and fear. I could not allow myself to participate in the creation of an image that would negatively affect my life. I decided to purposely think good thoughts, imagine good outcomes, speak good words, hear good reports, and see with my physical eyes good images throughout the entire day so that they would be imprinted on my subconscious mind and produce good results.

I began to ask myself, "If this thought, image, or word manifested in my life, would I be pleased?" I learned to challenge everything that entered my mind or issued from my mouth in order to discern if I wanted it imprinted on my subconscious or not. I avoided the things I did not desire and immersed myself in the things I did desire so as to ensure they were imprinted on my subconscious.

In this pursuit, God revealed to me the key to life. Indeed, what I have just explained to you is the same principle Jesus spoke of in Mark 4, a process commonly known as seedtime and harvest – whatever you plant will grow.

Now you may be asking, "What does this have to do with finding a wife?" I'm glad you asked.

In our quest for a wife, we must undertake our journey with the right mindset. How we view ourselves on this journey determines the results we get. Our mind functions as the compass for our lives, directing us on a course either to or away from our destiny. If we think in line with God's Word, our mind will produce results in line with God's Word, leading us closer to our destiny. Negative thoughts will produce opposite results. Keep in mind what the Bible says:

...as a man thinks in his heart so is he.
(Prov 23:7)

What does that tell us?

Well, it tells me what I put in my heart determines the way I think, which determines the way I speak. And that, ultimately, determines the condition of my life (Prov 4:23; Mt 12:33-37). If I do not like the condition of my life, I must first change the condition of my thoughts (Rom 12:2; 3 Jhn 2). For, if I have a wrong mindset, it will block what God wills to do in my life (Mt 13:58). By allowing God to open the eyes of my understanding (so that I see as He sees), He embeds an image into my soul (2 Kngs. 6:15-17). When that image is more real to me than my present surroundings, then nothing will be impossible to me. Because what's in me in abundance is flowing out of me to recreate, in the physical realm, what's in my heart through thoughts, words, and images (Gen 11:1-4; Prov 4:23; Prov 23:7; Mt 12:33-37).

Again, if our thoughts are positive, they lead to positive results. Meanwhile, negative thoughts set us in opposition to what we desire. It is like having our hands balled into fists. Even if someone wanted to give us something, they could not, because our hands are closed and not open to receive. This principle works in every arena of life, even in our search for the wives God has for us.

What are some examples of wrong thinking that could negatively affect our ability to receive from God the virtuous wives He intends for us to have?

- Women don't like me as much as the next guy.
- He's better than me.
- I'm not good enough. What do I have to offer?
- Most women are stupid whores and golddiggers.
- Valentine's Day was created by women and jewelry stores as a way to get your money.
- It's hard for me to be faithful.
- I'm still upset with Kelly for hurting me.
- Why am I doing this for Tasha when I didn't treat Amber right? After all, she was a good woman and deserved it.
- Sometimes, I can't stand Patricia.
- My mom is so annoying.

All of these represent thoughts that set us in opposition to what we desire to achieve. It is absolutely vital that we change our negative thoughts, words, and images, and allow ourselves to produce the life God has for us.

But, how do we do this?

The disciples basically asked the same question. They asked why they were not able to cast out the demon responsible for the little boy's illness. Jesus responded:

> Because of your unbelief; for assuredly, I say to you, if you had faith as a mustard seed, you will say to this mountain, 'move from here to there', and it will move; and nothing will be impossible to you. However this kind [of belief] does not go out except by prayer and fasting.
>
> Mt 17:20-21

So we change what's in our hearts by:

Taking the seed of faith, which is the Word of God, and planting it in our hearts through what we:

- see with our physical eyes
- say with our mouths
- hear with our ears
- think (thoughts and imaginations)
- do (what we do creates habits; our habits create us)

Guarding our hearts – where we've planted that precious seed – by monitoring what we:

- see with our physical eyes
- say with our mouths
- hear with our ears
- think
- do

If we continue on, we will see a change of what's in our hearts in abundance.

Thirty-fold if we give 30% of our hearts to change. Sixty-fold if we give 60% of our hearts to change. A hundred-fold if we give 100% of our hearts to change.

Remember, your heart is always working to produce the life you fill it with. Do you want your heart to produce:

- 30% God and 70% failure and defeat?
- 60% God and 40% broke, busted, and disgusted?
- 100% God and 100% victory?

This very principle was used by Abraham.

> He did not waver at the promise of God through unbelief, but was strengthened in faith, giving glory to God, and being fully convinced that what He had promised He was also well able to perform. And therefore, it was accounted to him for righteousness.
>
> Rom 4:20-22

When God promised Abraham that He would multiply his descendants as the stars of the heaven and as the sand on the seashore (Gen 15·5-6), Abraham meditated on that word day and night, by constantly looking at the stars and sand, speaking that word, hearing that word, and pondering that word, until he became strong enough to act in accordance with that word (Jos 1:8).

God called this process 'righteousness'. At its base, righteousness is being in agreement with God. And Abraham decided to agree with God by lining up his words, thoughts, images and actions with the words God had spoken. Therefore, he had a right to expect change. In Gen 22:1-14, we see evidence of three changes that took place because of his meditation.

He became quick to obey
He possessed new thoughts and images
He spoke differently.

When we meditate in the Word until it moves us to quick obedience, changes our thoughts and images, and changes our speech ('...for the righteousness of faith speaks in this way' [Rom 10:9]) then nothing will be impossible to us, because we act out on what we believe. However, if we choose to remain in fear, we will be like Job.

> For the thing I greatly feared has come upon me; and what I dreaded has happened to me.
>
> Job 3:25

I don't know about you, but I choose to believe. So let's set the compass.

It Is Not Good That Man Should Be Alone

In setting the compass of our minds to find the wives that God has for us, we must understand four truths.

1. It is God's will for you to be married.

If you have picked up this book, you probably have a God-given desire to be married. The good news is He wants, and designed for you to be married.

> And the Lord God said, "it is
> not good that man should be alone; I will make him a
> helper comparable to him."
>
> Gen 2:18

God has promised to make a helper 'comparable' to you. That word expresses someone 'suitable, designed for purpose, suitable for comparison, or similar and like.' So you can see from that definition, God is sending you someone on the same level as you.

What level have you attained to in your thinking? To the degree you've progressed is all that you can expect to be brought to you. Luke 6:38 presents it this way:

> ...for with the same measure
> you use, it will be measured back to you.

Remember, your heart is always producing according to what it is full of (Prov 4:23). The type of car you drive, you financial picture, your career, friendships, health, wife, and anything else flow out of your heart according to what you believe. Your master set of thoughts causes everything in your life to line up with it, producing according to its quality (3 Jhn 2).

Take inventory of your life. If you do not change anything, the only wife you can draw is someone with a similar set of life circumstances to yours.

Think about the parable of the talents in matt. 25:14-30. There the man gave talents to his three servants 'according to his own ability.' And it's amazing they performed just like he thought they would. Likewise, God will not give you a five talent wife if you are a two talent man. Nor, will He give you a two talent wife if you are a one talent man.

Is God playing favorites?

No. It is not Him who determines what you receive. It is you.

...for as he thinks in his heart, so is he.
Prov 23:7

That's why it's important for you to surround yourself with people who believe as you believe, or as you desire to believe. Because your heart will produce either the life God has for you, or the life Satan has for you.

But, what about those relationships where the two individuals do not appear to be on the same level?

Well, in those cases, one or both of them made a decision to enter that relationship because of an unseen commonality that is drawing them together – such as lust, fear, hurt, or loneliness. But, these relationships are not of God, as He instructs us not to be unequally yoked together with unbelievers (2 Cor 6:14).

Not only should you not enter into unions with those who are not born again, but also those who don't have the same master set of thoughts you do.

Just because someone is born again does not mean they have renewed their way of thinking (Rom 12:3). And un-renewed thinking can, sometimes, be worse than non-Christian thinking, because their long-held traditions and beliefs from wrong teaching robs them of the true power of God (Mt 13:58).

Understand, God's will is not just for you to be married, but for you to have a comparable wife with whom you share the same vision, without one dissenting voice of unbelief, so you can accomplish anything (Gen 11:6).

2. The wife you select will have a tremendous impact on the type of life you lead.

> As iron sharpens
> iron, so a man sharpens the countenance of his friend.
> Prov 27:17

It is absolutely vital that you realize that not only will you shape the thoughts of your future wife, but she also will shape your thoughts, desires, and course of action in life.

Many times we like to fancy ourselves as autonomous individuals: masters of our universe, independent from others. But, what does Amos 3:3 say?

> Can two walk together, unless they are agreed?

If you desire a successful marriage, you have to come to an agreement on several key issues in order to have peace. Failure to do so creates misery. If you are like most people, you hate misery, which means you'll try to make some adjustments to, at least, reach a place of comfort. This requires a meeting of the minds between you and your wife. This is the process in which you meld your ideas together. The question is...

Will those adjustments lead you to or away from God's will for your life? Look at Prov 31:10-11, 23 & 26:

v.10-11
> Who can find a virtuous
> wife? For her worth is far above rubies. The heart of
> her husband safely trust her; so he will have **no lack**
> **of gain**.

---

v.23

Her husband is known in
the gates, when he sits among the elders of the land.

v.26

She opens her mouth with
wisdom, and on her tongue is the law of kindness.

Notice she opens her mouth with wisdom, which means she meditated in that wisdom until she became full of it: "*...for out of the abundance of the heart the mouth speaks...*" (Matt 12:34). Therefore, she is now able to bring forth the same benefits as wisdom.

Prov 8:15

By me kings reign and rulers decree justice.

v.20-21

I traverse [walk about] the way
of righteousness, in the midst of the paths of justice,
that I may cause those who love me to inherit wealth,
that I may fill their treasuries.

v.35

For whoever find me finds life,
and obtains favor from the Lord.

Choose a wife of wisdom and she will lead you to the will of God for your life. But, what happens when you do not choose a wife in line with God's word? Invariably, she will turn you off course from the will of God for your life.

...and when the Lord your
God delivers them over to you, you shall conquer them
and utterly destroy them. You shall make no covenant
with them.
Nor shall you make marriages with them. You
shall not give your daughter to their son, nor take their
daughter for your son.

> For they will turn your sons away
> from following me, to serve other gods; so the anger of
> the Lord will be aroused against you and destroy you
> suddenly.
>
> Deu 7:2-4

> For a harlot is a deep pit, and
> a seductress is a narrow well. She also lies in wait as
> *for* a victim, and increases the unfaithful among men.
>
> Prov 23:27-28

The word 'for' is in italics; meaning it was added by privilege of the translator. Therefore, it can be read, 'She waits as a victim.' She is not looking for a victim. She *is* a victim.

Many times you think you're helping this woman. You may feel that you are her knight in shining armor. There is just something about her that draws you to her. You know she's not exactly what you want from God, but you just can't put your finger on it. I'll tell you what it is...

It's her weakness!

Every victim has a weakness. It is that which is flowing out of her heart in abundance. It is a homing signal calling out to anyone looking for it. It is creating her life. When you respond to her weakness, it is because of your weakness and that becomes the commonality around which this illicit affair is bound.

That's all a harlot is: someone who is involved in a relationship outside the bounds of covenant.

You have a covenant of marriage. Any intimate relationship outside of that covenant violates that covenant. You have now committed harlotry.

You have a covenant with God. An intimate relationship outside of that covenant (or his will for your life) violates that covenant. You have now committed harlotry.

In Ezekiel 23:1-49, we see an allegory of Samaria and Jerusalem concerning their unfaithfulness towards God with other nations. God calls their wrong relationships harlotry. It is more than sexual sin. It is when we say to God, "I know you have a plan for my life. But, I value this non-God-authored relationship more than you."

Understand, where there is a relationship outside the bounds of your relationship with God, there is harlotry. Where there is harlotry, there is an increase of unfaithfulness.

So, what happens in these relationships?

You both end up hurt (Eze 23:17 & 22-26), because this was not a relationship based on God's covenant.

> ...therefore what God has joined together, let not man separate.
>
> Mt 19:6

You must be after what God has joined together, or else the relationship lacks the power to endure. That's why choosing a wife of wisdom is vitally important.

But, where does a wife of wisdom come from?

> Houses and riches are an inheritance from fathers, but a prudent wife is from the Lord.
>
> Prov 19:14

You can receive many things through natural means: houses, money, cars, careers. But, one thing that no one on earth can give you is a prudent wife. It is through submission to His way that we are able to receive one of His greatest gifts. After all, Jeremiah 31:22 tells us, *"...a woman shall encompass a man."*

That word 'encompass' means to: turn, turn around, turn back or towards, surround, change direction, transform, envelop, reverse, enclose, cause to turn.

God is using woman to help shape your course and bring you about into a man (a champion, a mighty man, a man in all his strength).

3. **You should never be in such a hurry to be married that you are willing to replace what God designed for your life with an imitation. Doing so has lifelong ramifications.**

The best example of this is Abraham. God promised Abraham a son. However, his wife, Sarah, was barren. But, we know that

"...with God nothing shall be impossible" (Lk 1:37). Yet, Abraham was so anxious for the promise of God to come to pass that he heeded the voice of his wife when she suggested he sleep with her servant to produce a son.

Abraham did not heed the voice of God, because he looked at his circumstances and thought, "no way can this happen with my wife and me. Maybe this is the way God intends for this to happen."

In his haste, Abraham failed to seek God concerning how this was to happen. You must be careful not to miss the rest of the message, choosing, instead to listen to someone not familiar with the promise, because, *God did not speak it to them.*

All you will have accomplished is creating difficulties for yourself because:

    a) Your Ishmael (substitute) and your Isaac (promise) will
       never mesh.

    b) They will always be at war.

Why? Because the two were never meant to coexist. They were of two different seeds. One was of the seed of faith, and the other was of the seed of fear.

Even till this day, the descendants of Isaac (Israel) and the descendants of Ishmael (Arab nations) are still at war; for the seed produces after its kind. If your wife is not born of the seed of faith, the seed (or works) she produces will always work to short-circuit the vision you're working to accomplish.

Only that which is born of faith can produce the promise. That which is born of fear will only produce a facsimile.

4. God is ready when you are.

We've all said it before: "Well, I guess it's not time for me to get married."

But, is that true? What if He was waiting on you to receive His word and act on it? In Is 48:3, God says:

> I have declared the
> former things from the beginning; they went forth from
> my mouth, and I caused them to hear it. Suddenly I did
> them, and they came to pass.

What thing has He already declared?

> And the Lord said, "It is
> not good that man should be alone. I will make him a
> helper comparable to him."
>
> Gen 2:18

The way I see it, God has already declared everything in your life. However, it has a sequence that must be followed in order to see it take place in your life.

Imagine you are playing a game where one task leads you to the next task, which leads you to the next task until you find the prize. If you only read the first task and stop there, you will never get to the task which leads you to the prize.

Or, picture an educational curriculum that was already printed before you started school. How silly would you sound if you blamed the superintendent because you couldn't hear the words designed for a twelfth grade student if you refused to progress past the fourth grade?

Likewise, God has given you a series of tasks pertaining to the grade level you are in. Once you complete those tasks, you move to the next grade level where there is a new set of tasks, a new set of words, a new set of manifestations. Therefore, it is not God who determines when you hear the words He has already spoken from the beginning. It is *you* through *your* progression. So the question is: How do you progress?

> ...if you have faith as a mustard seed...
>
> Mt 17:20

> But these are the ones
> sown on good ground, those who hear the word, accept
> it, and bear fruit: some thirtyfold, some sixty, and some
> a hundred.
>
> Mk 4:20

You progress by taking His word, putting it in your heart, and meditating on that word until you 'observe' to do it (Jos 1:8). And, eventually, it will produce manifestation.

God has given you every word for your life as a seed (Gen 1:29). The life you are looking to obtain, you already possess. So now, prepare and progress.

Saturate Yourself With the Word of God For Your Life

> Keep your heart with all
> diligence for out of it spring the issues of life.
>
> Prov 4:23

> ... for out of the abundance of
> the heart, the mouth speaks.
>
> Mt 12:34

From these two scriptures you can see it clearly stated that from your heart flow the forces that shape your life. But it isn't just what you put in your heart – it's what you put in your heart in abundance.

The life you live has been dictated by what you have put into your heart. Therefore, you must be diligent to make sure what comes out of you is the life God has for you. In order to do this, you must saturate your heart with God's specific word and plan for your life.

> Till I come, give attention to reading, to exhortation, to doctrine. Do not neglect the gift that is in you, which, was given to you by prophecy with the laying on of the hands of the eldership. Meditate on these things; give yourself entirely to them, that your progress may be evident to all. Take heed to yourself and to the doctrine. Continue in them, for in doing this you will save both yourself and those who hear you.
>
> 1 Tim 4:13-16

Inside of every man is a gift [a gift of grace, a free gift, a miraculous faculty, a divine gratuity, a spiritual endowment] that comes from God. His intention is for you to use this enablement that is specific to you to change lives.

When you meditate on and give yourself entirely to it, along with readings, exhortation, and doctrine, the progress you make in life becomes evident, or seen by all. It is by this commitment that you can finally live the life God intended. In addition to perfecting yourself, you're also perfecting others.

So, how do you discover the specific word for your life?

> He who has my commandments
> and keeps them, it is he who loves Me. And he who
> loves Me will be loved by My Father, and I will love
> him and manifest Myself to him.
>
> Jhn 14:21

> When Christ who is
> our life appears, then you also will appear with Him
> in glory.
>
> Col 3:4

You may not have a clue as to why you were born in this earth. But if you will keep His word or commandments, eventually He will manifest in your life. And when He appears, who you are cannot help but be revealed with Him.

It goes back to the principle of seedtime and harvest. Jesus said, *"Keep My word"* (Jhn 14:23). In Lk 8:11, it says:

> Now the parable is this: The seed is the Word of God.

So, you are taking His word as a seed, and planting it in the ground of your heart. You keep that seed until you bring forth a harvest (lk 8:15). Some of you will bring forth a thirtyfold harvest, some a sixtyfold, and some a hundredfold (Mk 4:20), according to how each man farmed. When you bring forth a harvest, the life of that seed appears; is seen and manifested.

In John 1:1, it reads:

In the beginning was the word,
and the word was with God, and the Word was God.

v.14

And the Word became flesh...

When you keep His word, you are taking Jesus into the ground of your heart, and cracking Him open, and bringing forth the different elements of who He is. That's what Mary did. The angel, Gabriel, spoke a word to her that she would bring forth a son, and call His name Jesus (lk 1:31). She received that word as a seed into the ground of her heart by responding, *"Let it be according to your word"* (lk 1:38). And nine months later, we see the life of that seed through the physical birth of Jesus.

That word carried with it the power to reveal life. Encoded in that word was a purpose, a plan, the color of His hair, His friends, His career, His mannerisms, His house; all that was His life.

So, what does that have to do with you?

Well, it has been shown through scripture that Jesus is nothing more than words. That's why the scripture says he is *'...upholding all things by the word of His power'* (Heb 1:3), because that's who He is. Likewise, we are nothing more than words.

In Gen 1, God spoke words:

v.26

...Let Us make man...

Next, He speaks concerning how man should be, how he should operate, and what he is to possess.

v.26

...Let Us make man in our image, after Our likeness...

v.28-29

Then God blessed them, and God said to them, "Be fruitful and multiply; fill the earth and subdue it; have dominion over the fish of the sea, over the birds of the air, and over every living thing that moves on the earth." And God said, "See, I have given you every herb that yields seed which is on the face of all the earth, and every tree whose fruit yields seed; to you it shall be for food..."

Last, He forms man's body of the dust of the ground, and breathes into man's nostril's the breath of life, or his spirit containing words. Just like your physical body is dust at its base, your spirit is simply words. These words contain every detail about your life.

However, the Bible doesn't speak about the specifics of your life. So, where does that leave you?

For you died, and your life is
hidden with Christ in God.

Col 3:3

Because your life is hidden with Christ in God, the only way for you to find out the specifics of your life is to allow Jesus' word to be manifested in your life. That word, who is Jesus, contains the master set of instructions for your heart's ground on how to produce a harvest of the seed of that word, which was breathed into your nostrils on the day you were born.

Think of yourself as a computer. Your soul, or heart, is the processor that reads the information and runs the program. Your body is just the physical casing. And your spirit is the software. If the processor does not receive the correct instructions or is infected with a virus, it cannot properly run the program it received for the software.

But, if you give your processor the correct instructions – the Bible (basic instructions before leaving earth) – and if you remove all the viruses (the cares of this world, the deceitfulness of riches, etc. [Mk 4:19]), your processor can properly run the program it received from the software.

By receiving God's written word, you are training your heart to make known His spoken word, which is your spirit. And when you hear a word (Is 30:21), it's that 'breathed in' word (Gen 2:7) speaking to you.

Look at Jhn 14:20:

> At that day [the day you keep
> and manifest His word] you will know that I am in My
> Father, and you in Me, and I in you.

What is He saying?

He's saying, "I am of the seed that has power to reveal life. If you get in Me, and put Me in you, then you are of the seed that reveals life."

As your purpose begins to be revealed and you begin to walk according to the specific word for your life, you will find the scriptures you were studying beforehand will begin to produce results where there previously were not any results.

You can study scriptures on prosperity, healing and deliverance, determining to put it in your heart and produce a harvest. However, you will see minimal results until you begin to walk according to the purpose for your life. All of the scriptures you've been studying need a place to get involved; an avenue by which to flow. And your purpose is the conduit of blessings. Remember what 1 Tim 4:13-16 says: it's when you give yourself entirely to what God has committed to you that your progress is evident to all, and you can now be of benefit to others.

Adam was able to be of benefit as long as he was walking in his purpose. In Gen 2, God placed Adam in the Garden, the place he specifically designed for Adam to be. There, He instructed Adam to tend, or cultivate, and keep the Garden.

So, likewise, there are some things designed by God, specifically, for you. But, in order to see them manifested in your life, you're going to have to spend some time cultivating and developing these things. You cannot be afraid to put forth the labor you were created for. You must respond like Adam did.

How did he respond? He became that word. What word?

> Be fruitful and multiply; fill the
> earth and subdue it, have dominion over the fish of the
> sea, over the birds of the air, and over every living thing
> that moves on the earth.
>
> Gen 1:28

> Then the Lord God took
> the man and put him in the garden of Eden to tend and
> keep it. and the Lord God commanded the man saying,
> "Of every tree of the Garden you may freely eat; but
> of the tree of the knowledge of good and evil you shall
> not eat, for in the day that you eat of it you shall surely
> die." And the Lord God said, "It is not good that man
> should be alone; I will make him a helper comparable
> to him."
>
> Gen 2:15-18

He was diligent about keeping that word because in the very next scripture we see Adam giving names to all of the creatures God formed. So, now, through Adam, you can see being full of God's word for your life affords you three benefits.

1. The Word of God for your life allows you to judge everything according to your purpose.

In Gen 2:20, we see Adam is now walking according to that word of his life: his purpose.

> So Adam gave names to all
> cattle, to the birds of the air, and to every beast of
> the field. But for Adam there was not found a helper
> comparable to him.

As he is walking according to his purpose, he is judging everything that is before him to see if it is comparable, or suitable, for him. What was he using as the criteria to determine whether or not something was suitable for him?

The Word of God, his purpose, or the blueprint for his life.

When you are saturated with God's word for your life, you have a set of blueprints that tells you how your life should look. It also tells you what materials you need, and the personnel required to get the job done.

So, now every time you meet a young lady, you are able to ask and answer the question: Is this person suitable for my purpose? Remember:

As iron sharpens iron, so a man
sharpens the countenance of his friend.

Prov 27:17

That's important to remember. Because if she is not suitable, she can be nothing more than a hindrance to you fulfilling your purpose. It doesn't mean she is a bad person. It simply means she can't understand where you are destined to go and what you are to accomplish.

Do not be fooled by her exuberance for your plans. She is excited about your potential for greatness. She sees the blueprints, but she does not understand how to recreate the image. Or, she may not understand the image at all, because she was not equipped for the purpose.

For example, when I first joined World Changers Ministry, there were pictures and a model of the new church we were to build. Every member understood what they were seeing – a church – but, hardly any of us were equipped to take the blueprints and build the church. We could see it, but couldn't fulfill it. However, some can't even understand what they see.

In 1996, I was on the train a few weeks before the Olympics. On the train were two women who obviously didn't come into the city often. And as we passed the newly built high-rise Fulton County jail, one lady said to the other, "Look, they are building all of these nice new buildings for the Olympics." She could see the building, but she had no idea what it was. It reminds me of Mark 4:11-12.

And he said to them, "To you it
has been given to know the mystery of the kingdom of
God; but to those who are outside, all things come in
parables, so that 'seeing they may see and not perceive,
and hearing they may hear and not understand...'"

Realize, not everyone is going to understand your purpose. They are not trying to be difficult. But, without the call, which brings the equipment, they can't follow you. And, what you are looking for is someone who can see you, while being equipped to bring *you* forth.

> My beloved is white
> and ruddy, chief among ten thousand. His head is like
> the finest gold; his locks are wavy, and black as a
> raven. His eyes are like doves by the rivers of waters
> washed with milk, and fitly set. His cheeks are like
> a bed of spices, banks of scented herbs. His lips are
> lilies, dripping   liquid myrrh. His hands are rods of
> gold set with beryl. His body is carved ivory inlaid
> with sapphires. His legs are pillars of marble set on
> bases of fine gold. His countenance is like Lebanon,
> excellent as the cedars. His mouth is most sweet, yes,
> he is altogether lovely. This is my friend, o daughters of
> Jerusalem.
>
> Song 5:10-16

Here we see a woman who has vision to see who her beloved is and what he is to accomplish. But, it doesn't stop there. She is also equipped to bring Him forth. This is apparent because she is able to recognize and speak eloquently of the different elements that comprise the finished picture.

The journey is about looking for a wife who can see what you see, believe what you believe, and understand what you understand.

> And they said, "Come, let us
> build ourselves a city, and a tower whose top is in the
> heavens; let us make a name for ourselves, lest we be
> scattered abroad over the face of the whole earth."
> But the Lord came down to see the city and tower
> which the sons had built. And the Lord said, "Indeed
> the people are one and they all have one language, and
> this is what they begin to do; now nothing that they
> propose to do will be withheld from them."
>
> Gen 11 4-6

Notice, they had one language and one speech. There was not a dissenting voice of unbelief among them. Therefore, when you find a

---

wife with whom you can be of one accord, nothing will be withheld from you. However, you can only find this type of relationship when you are saturated with the word of God for your life.

2. It hastens the arrival of your spouse

Gen 2:16

> And the Lord God commanded the man, saying, "of every tree in the Garden you may freely eat."

v.18

> And the Lord God said, "It is not good that man should be alone; I will make him a helper comparable to him."

Notice, God spoke a word about a wife at the same time he spoke Adam's purpose. In Gen 1:27, it says:

> ...male and female He created them.

v.28

> Then God blessed *them,* and God said to *them...*

Eve was a part of the required personnel according to the blueprints of Adam's life. She was written on every page just like Adam, for they shared the same purpose. We don't see Eve right away, because Adam had to become full of the word concerning a wife, meditating and pondering what would be suitable. At the moment he became full, God allowed him to dream.

> And the Lord God caused a deep sleep to fall on Adam, and he slept; and he took one of his ribs, and closed up the flesh in its place.
>
> Gen 2:21

Why?

If the clouds are full of rain,
they empty themselves upon the earth;
Ecc 11:3

A good man out of the good
treasure of his heart brings forth good things...
Mt 12:35

Because, what he was full of had to come out of him. God was confident the image Adam would dream, or produce, would be in line with the purpose He had for him. Adam meditated in that word until it shaped his desire.

Delight [make pliable] yourself
also in the Lord, and He shall give [put in] you the
desires of your heart.
Ps 37:4

Adam's desire was active while he slept.

My root is spread out to
the waters, and the dew lies all night on my branch
[process of harvesting].
Job 29:19

And while he slept, his desire was producing images that would flow out of his heart as a harvest. Because, the heart never stops producing what it is full of. Once, he produced the image that was Eve, God was able to take out his rib and create, or build, Eve.

Then the rib which the
Lord God had taken from man He made into a woman,
and He brought her to the man.
Gen 2:22

What was Adam's response?

V.23

This is now bone of my bones
and flesh of my flesh; she shall be called woman,
because she was taken out of man.

Adam was not surprised to see her, because she looked just like the image he was dreaming of.

Now, what did God use to build woman?

- The rib
- The blueprint
- The purpose
- The Word of God
- The wisdom for Adam's life

The wife you are to have shall come out of the desires and the imaginations; the substance of your heart.

> For a man indeed ought not
> cover his head, since he is the image and glory of God;
> but woman is the glory of man.
>
> 1 Cor 11:7

That word 'glory' is used primarily when talking about the nature and acts of God in self-manifestation, i.e., what He essentially is and does, as exhibited in whatever way He reveals Himself.

Man is the self-manifestation of God. And when you bring forth a wife from your heart, you have revealed what is in you – who you are. Everything you need to know about a man you can tell by looking at his wife.

> ...and they shall become one flesh.
>
> Gen 2:24b

> Nevertheless, neither is man
> independent of woman, nor is woman independent of
> man, in the Lord. For as woman came from man, even
> so man also comes through woman; but all things are
> from God.
>
> 1 Cor 11:11-12

God's intent is for you to bring forth a wife out of the design of His purpose for your life and then bring you into the fullness of your purpose through your wife. But, you must fill up like a cloud and dream.

3. It allows you to give your wife a rib that is saturated with the Word of God for your life

The clearer you are about your purpose, the easier it will be for her to help you with your vision.

If you are only 25% full of your purpose, she can only help you with 25% of your vision.

If you are only 50% full of your purpose, she can only help you with 50% of your vision.

If you are 100% full of your purpose, she can help you bring to pass everything God has designed.

That rib plays a crucial role in the preparedness of your wife to assist you. However, it does not mean she will be perfect. But, she will be thoroughly equipped to deal with you. Because, when she received your rib, she received your spiritual DNA.

Therefore, when your wife is manifested, do not compartmentalize her, thinking she is a separate entity from your vision, as if it's yours and only yours. For:

She is not a part of the purpose.
She is not a benefit of the purpose.
She *is* the purpose manifested.

She was spoken at the same time as the rest of God's word for your life.

Gen 1:27
...male and female He created them.'

v.28
Then God blessed them, and God said to them...

Notice, she received the same call. What you must understand is your wife has been called according to the purpose, not to the man. And, when you are full of the Word of God for your life, it will lead you to the woman who was called according to your purpose.

One Blessing. Three Women.

This is clearly illustrated by looking at the fathers of our faith. The purpose on Abraham's life brought him a wife, Sarah. She was a woman of beautiful countenance chosen to bear the promised seed of Abraham (Gen 12:11).

The purpose on Isaac's life brought to him Rebekah, whose name describes a woman so beautiful she could captivate men. It was also illustrated that she was a diligently industrious and beautifully sensitive girl (Gen 24:4, 12-15).

The purpose on Jacob's life brought to him Rachel, a beautiful shepherdess.

These women were very similar in many different ways and experienced similar situations.

a. They were all beautiful. So much so that Sarah and Rebekah had to pretend to be their husbands' sisters for their welfare (Gen 12:10-20; 26:6-14)

b. They all tried to obtain blessings through natural means. Rebekah and Rachel even deceived the men in their own households (Gen 16:1-2; 27:1-29; 31:19-35)

c. They all displayed an aspect of seedtime and harvest:
   • Sarah was chosen to bear the seed (Gen 17:15-16)
   • Rebekah watered the seed (Gen 24:15-20)
   • Rachel nurtured the seed (Gen 29:9)

What was the common denominator that brought these men the same type of woman and how did they find them?

> ...blessing I will bless you [Abraham] and multiplying I will multiply your descendants as the stars of the heaven and as the sand which is on the seashore; and your descendants shall possess the gates of their enemies. In your seed all the nations of the earth shall be blessed, because you have obeyed my voice.
>
> Gen 22:17-18

And I will make your [Isaac]
descendants multiply as the stars of the heaven; I will
give to your descendants all these lands; and in your
seed all the nations of the earth shall be blessed.

Gen 26:4

For you said, 'I will surely
treat you [Jacob] well, and make your descendants
as the sand of the sea, which cannot be numbered for
multitude.'

Gen 32:12

The common denominator was the blessing, which they continually meditated upon. That was how they found their wives. You don't seek a wife by dating woman after woman. You find your wife through meditation of God's word. Seek your wife through the scriptures.

Develop
A Relationship
With Wisdom

> Houses and riches are an
> inheritance from fathers, but a prudent wife is from
> the Lord.
>
> Prov 19:14

If you desire a prudent wife, you must go about receiving her through the ways that God has established, for He is the only one who can bring to you a wife of wisdom. But how do you prepare for a wife of wisdom?

By developing a relationship with wisdom.

Throughout the Bible, there are strong correlations between a virtuous, prudent wife and wisdom.

> For whoever finds me [wisdom]
> finds life, and obtains favor from the Lord.
>
> Prov 8:35

> He who finds a wife finds a
> good thing; and obtains favor from the Lord.
>
> Prov 18:22

> For wisdom is better than
> rubies, and all the things one may desire cannot be
> compared with her.
>
> Prov 8:11

Who can find a virtuous wife?
For her worth is far above rubies.

Prov 31:10

Wisdom has built her house...

Prov 9:1

The wise woman builds her house...

Prov 14:1

When a woman submits herself to the power of God, she becomes wisdom, taking on wisdom's characteristics. That's why wisdom is spoken of in the feminine. God wants you to understand clearly that when you marry a virtuous, prudent wife, you have married a woman who has become wisdom and brings all of wisdom's benefits.

If the ax is dull, and one does not sharpen the edge, then he must use more strength; but wisdom brings success.

Ecc 10:10

"Then I [wisdom] was beside Him as a master craftsman..."

Prov 8:30

A wife of wisdom is able to bring you sweatless success where you were previously struggling, because she is a master craftsman; she was created to create. And, everything you were praying to see in your life comes into existence through her.

Now, that's exciting. But, if you're like me, you're saying, "That's great. But, how does that benefit me? I'm a single man. Am I forced to struggle until marriage?"

The answer to that question was spoken as I studied Gen 2:22.

Then the rib which the Lord God had taken from man he made into a woman, and He brought her to the man.

At that moment, I heard wisdom say, "I've got you." And the light bulb went off. The very same wisdom that is on your future wife to take care of you is the very same wisdom you already possess.

> Drink water from your own
> cistern, and running water from your own well.
>
> Prov 5:15

> The words of a man's mouth
> are deep waters; the wellspring of wisdom is a flowing
> brook.
>
> Prov 18:4

On the inside of every man is wisdom that is specific for his life. When you give to your wife your rib, you have given to her the equipment and the specific set of instructions – the operating manual – to care for and deal with you.

Wisdom, therefore, wants you to develop a relationship with her and depend on her long before you meet your wife. The question now becomes:

"How do I develop a relationship with wisdom?"

Well, in order to develop a relationship with wisdom, you must be where wisdom is. You must go where she is going. You have to find her at the place where she operates.

> I traverse the way
> of righteousness, in the midst of the paths of justice...
>
> Prov 9:20

Once you begin to walk in righteousness, wisdom is now able to aid you. Wisdom walks about the righteousness you operate in. She traverses, courses, or moves back and forth across the images and thoughts you have on the inside, as well as the words you speak out of your mouth. Why?

> That I may cause those
> who love me to inherit wealth, that I may fill their
> treasuries.
>
> Prov 9:21

Wisdom is moving back and forth across your righteousness to see how she can be of benefit to you, helping you bring to pass what you believe – your images, thoughts, and speech. Wisdom is functioning as a consultant, helping you develop that inner image. She develops you through righteousness and enables you to walk perfectly in it. She does this by teaching you how to talk, act, think, and by shaping your desires, knowing what flows out of your heart in abundance is what you will see in your physical life.

> Listen, for I will speak of excellent things, and from the opening of my lips will come right things for my mouth will speak truth; wickedness is an abomination to my lips. All the words of my mouth are with righteousness; nothing crooked or perverse is in them. They are all plain to him who understands, and right to those who find knowledge.
>
> Prov 8:6-9

> Now therefore, listen to me [wisdom], my children. For blessed are those who keep my ways.
>
> Prov 8:32

When you allow wisdom to develop you in righteousness, she can now function in her other capacity as a master craftsman. This means she is no longer just helping you develop your inner image, but also actively constructing that image in your physical life. She is taking the issues of life, or the faith, flowing out of your heart and using them as the material with which to build what you see.

> Exalt her, and she will promote you; she will bring you honor, when you embrace her. She will place on your head an ornament of grace; a crown of glory she will deliver to you.
>
> Prov 4:8-9

And, all the while, she will be instructing you as to where you should go to locate the manifestation of your image.

When you roam, they
[commandments] will lead you; when you sleep, they
will keep you; and when you awake, they will speak
with you.

Prov 6:22

As long as you stay in righteousness, you can have a relationship with wisdom, as she can shape your thoughts, dreams, speech, and actions, while also making provisions for you. The moment you step outside of righteousness – by acting, thinking, speaking, or imagining contrary to God's Word – you sever your relationship with wisdom. For it's when you get in God's Word and begin to visualize His word in your life that wisdom can go to work bringing that image to pass. How do you develop in your relationship with wisdom?

First, stay in righteousness!
Second, practice being accountable.
Third, make decisions with wisdom in mind.
Fourth, be pliable to wisdom.

Many times the thought of being single leads people to believe they answer to no one else and have only themselves to consider. However, if you're going to have a relationship with wisdom, there is an adjustment you will have to make. Because, when you value wisdom as a real person, you will understand she is deserving of the same consideration as any physical person.

When it comes to being accountable, imagine if I told you I would meet you at 8 o'clock in the morning, but never showed. How would you feel?

Likewise, how do you think wisdom feels when you make promises you don't keep?

You said you were going to pray in the morning.
You didn't.
You said you were going to tithe regularly.
You don't.
You said you were going to complete what God told you to do.
You didn't.
You said you were going to keep your house clean.
It's filthy.

You said you were going to be on time.
You're late.
You said you're going to be a better employee.
You're ineffective.
You said you're going to be consistent and/or dependable.
You're erratic.
Wisdom is trying to help you, but she can't if you're going to violate spiritual law and refuse to be faithful in what is least.

> He who is faithful in what is
> least is faithful also in much; and he who is unjust in
> what is least is unjust also in much.
>
> Lk 16:10

You must begin to make decisions with wisdom in mind. If you don't submit to wisdom, or get under her mission of helping you, then she cannot be of benefit to you. You must work in tandem. Therefore, you must stop thinking of yourself as an individual, and start thinking of yourself as a partnership.

Individuals make purchases on their own. Partners confer with each other.

Individuals view their actions only in light of how they affect them. Partners take the time to consider how their actions affect their partner.

Individuals stay out all night. Partners choose not to, so they won't worry their partners.

Understand, you are not in a relationship with a physical person. But, you are in a relationship. And, you are in relationship with someone whose value is far above rubies (prov 8:11). So, value it. Value it to the point where your time with her is important.

Too often, we, as men, fill up our time with idle relationships; having multiple women we can 'hang out' with. But, when you do that you've only impeded your relationship with wisdom, which should be the most valuable bond in your life.

In no way am I saying you cannot have female friendships or go out on dates to get to know someone. Just keep in mind that those idle relationships – or relationships that you've determined are going nowhere – are robbing you of an opportunity to spend time with wisdom.

If anyone is not adding to your life by bringing you closer to your destiny, then she is taking away from your life by halting your progress. Take heed that you let no one halt your progress, for that is the beginning of you falling back from your destiny.

> ...and let us **run** with endurance
> the race that is set before us...
>
> Heb 12:1b

> Blessed is the man who **walks**
> not in the counsel of the ungodly, nor **stands** in the
> path of sinners, nor **sits** in the seat of the scornful.
>
> Ps 1:1

> Therefore we must give the
> more earnest heed to the things we have heard, lest
> we **drift away**.
>
> Heb 2:1

Nothing stands still. Either you are moving in the direction of your destiny, or you are falling away from it. Initially, you're running towards your destiny. But, through idle relationships, you begin to walk   stand,,, sit. And, now that you are no longer giving proper consideration to the Word of God, you begin to drift away from your destiny to the old works of the flesh. It happened with Solomon. He forgot his relationship with wisdom, and idle relationships turned his heart from God.

> But King Solomon loved many
> foreign women, as well as the daughter of Pharaoh:
> women of the Moabites, Ammonites, Edomites,
> Sidonians, and Hittites.
>
> 1 Kngs 11:1

> For it was so, when Solomon
> was old that his wives turned his heart after other
> gods; and his heart was not loyal to the Lord his God,
> as was the heart of his father David.
>
> 1 Kngs 11:4

Who is impeding your relationship with wisdom? Who is hindering you from finding your wife? Let those idle relationships go. Do not use 'he that findeth a wife...' as justification for your harem, a harem that is used only to mask your insecurities. You do not find a wife by chasing woman after woman. You find her through the scriptures.

Find scriptures that are about a wife. Take those scriptures and put them in your heart through meditation and by standing on your righteousness. At that point, wisdom will move across your righteousness, developing you in that word – shaping your image and constructing your expectations – so she can bring into manifestation what you desire: A wife.

However, that requires time spent with wisdom, so she may not only shape your desires but prepare you as well.

Wisdom wants to talk with you, to tell you what she likes and dislikes. But, when she speaks, you must be pliable enough to listen to her and make the necessary corrections. Should wisdom tell you she disapproves of the movie you're watching, the music you're listening to, the words you're speaking, the friends you have, or even the food you're eating, be willing to make the adjustments. Wisdom is trying to inform you of things that are inhibiting her productivity in your relationship.

Establishing a relationship with wisdom is preparation for a relationship with your future wife. It is practice. However, it does not come without its own set of benefits. Rest assured, when you develop a relationship with wisdom, it brings four powerful benefits.

1. Wisdom will take care of you

Listen, for I will speak of excellent things,
and from the opening of my lips will come right things.

Prov 8:6

Come, eat of my bread and
drink of the wine I have mixed.

Prov 9:5

Love her and she will keep you.

Prov 4:6b

Exalt her and she will promote you...

Prov 4:8a

She is a tree of
life to those who take hold of her, and happy are all
who retain her.

Prov 3:18

Everything that a wife can do for you, wisdom wants to do for you now, while you're single. She will:

a. bring you wealth
b. bring you success
c. build you up and give you answers
d. make sure you have plenty of the best food to eat
e. watch over you
f. bring you promotion
g. cause you to be healthy and happy

Wisdom wants to help you cook, clean your home, dress yourself, do your daughter's hair if you're a single father. However, the reason you don't see the practical benefits of wisdom in your life is because you don't spend enough time developing a relationship with wisdom.

a. begin to seek after wisdom through prayer and study
b. have conversations with her
c. ask her for help with what you are doing

d. listen to her advice and submit, honoring her
e. thank her for her help
f. consult her when making decisions
g. avoid things she doesn't like, making changes at her request

When you do these things, you are training yourself to have a relationship with your wife. This brings about the second benefit of your relationship with wisdom.

2. It determines the relationship you have with your wife. It facilitates this relationship.

When you establish a relationship with your wife, it will mirror the relationship you have with wisdom. If you are used to seeking after wisdom, then you will naturally seek after your wife. To the degree you treasure, trust, yield to, and rely upon wisdom, so you will do with your wife.

Practicing a relationship with wisdom keeps you from having to make wholesale changes to accommodate your wife. As a result, you will not resist honoring her request, because you're already in the habit of yielding.

It becomes easier to love your wife, because you love wisdom.

It becomes easier to pursue your wife, because you pursue wisdom.

It becomes easier to listen to your wife, because you listen to wisdom.

What you do for wisdom, you'll do for your wife.

What you won't do for wisdom, you won't do for your wife.

Remember, the wisdom your future wife will possess in order to care for you is the same wisdom you presently possess. So, the value you attach to wisdom is the value you'll attach to your wife. Therefore, learning to value wisdom is crucial. For one day, wisdom will speak with the voice of your wife. And, if you value wisdom, you will value the word that comes out of her mouth.

She opens her mouth with wisdom...
Prov 31:26a

In order for you to get to the place God designed for you, you must value the words that come from your wife's mouth. God has promised you 'a land flowing with milk and honey' (Deu 6:3). But, do you know where the source of that honey is found?

> Moreover, He said to me,
> "son of man, eat what you find; eat this scroll, and go, speak to the house of Israel."
> So I opened my mouth, and He caused me to eat the scroll. And He said to me, "Son of man, feed your belly, and fill your stomach with this scroll that I give you."
> So I ate, and it was in my mouth like **honey** in sweetness. Then He said to me: "son of man, go to the house of Israel and speak with my words to them."
> Eze3:1-4

The source of that honey is the word of God that He intended to be released in your life through the speaking of those words. And when your wife opens her mouth, she becomes the pump for honey and milk to flow throughout your land.

> Your lips, o my spouse, drip as the honeycomb. Honey and milk are under your tongue...
> Song 4:11a

However, if you adhere to Prov 24:13-14, you can already experience that flow, now, as a single man, and be developed at valuing and submitting to that word.

> My son, eat honey because it is good. And the honeycomb which is sweet to your taste; so shall the knowledge of wisdom be to your soul. 'If you have found it, there is a prospect [reward]. And your hope will not be cut off.
> Prov 24:13-14

3. Wisdom heightens your love for your wife.

Remember, the more you love wisdom, the more you love your wife, because she has become that wisdom with whom you've so fully connected. It causes you to see her with different eyes. And, in spite of her imperfections, you begin to spew out praise on her.

> Her children rise up and call her blessed; her husband also and he praises her: "Many daughters have done well, but you excel them all."
>
> Prov 31:28-29

That's the reason why Adam didn't hate Eve, because she was precious to him. She possessed something that came out of him. And there was nothing she could do to cause him to turn his back on her. Truly a great love was born because wisdom was taken out of him and made manifest as Eve.

Imagine how you would feel if someone you loved helped convince you to sin against your father, separating you from all your inheritance and authority. And, now, you must slave by the sweat of your brow just to make ends meet. You went from being king to being a servant.

The anger that many of us would harbor in our hearts would be too great to overcome, but not for Adam. At that moment, it was what Paul spoke of concerning Jesus' love and faithfulness towards us in 2 Tim 2:13:

> If we are faithless,
> He remains faithful;
> He cannot deny Himself.

If Adam turned his back on Eve it, would have been similar to him turning his back on himself. And the love he had for the preciousness that came out of him overrode anything Eve could ever have done. Eve was the instrument Satan used to bring forth the death, or separation, of man's relationship with God. However, Adam chose to speak life and restoration unto her in Gen 3:20 by naming her Eve, or 'the mother of all living'. When he looked through the eyes of love, he saw her as she truly was, and not according to her past mistakes or flaws.

The mindset Adam possessed was not of his own doing. It was the divine design of God. He took the rib out of Adam and used it to make Eve so that he would love Eve unconditionally. As Mark 6:21 states:

> For where your treasure is, there your heart will be also.

Eve was Adam's treasure, so his heart had no other choice but to also be with Eve. As he was so saturated with the Word of God for his life that it coated his bones, he gave her the very essence of who he was and just a piece of him was able to transfer life to another being.

You may think I'm delusional, but this is clearly illustrated in the life of Elisha, one of God's prophets.

> So it was, as they were burying a man that suddenly they spied a band of raiders; and they put the man in the tomb of Elisha; and when the man was let down and touched the bones of Elisha, he revived and stood on his feet.
>
> 2 Kngs 13:24

Now why was this man able to be revived by the bones of Elisha?

> Thus says the Lord God to these bones: "Surely I will cause breath to enter into you, and you shall live."
>
> Eze 37:15

The man was able to be revived because of the breath of life, or the words, that came from the mouth of God. That word inhabited the bones of Elisha, just as it inhabited the bones of Adam, just as God wants it to inhabit and saturate your bones, so that he may take of your treasure and impart it into your wife.

...and receive with meekness the implanted word...

Jam. 1:21

Now, God is not going to take a physical rib out of you, but He is going to take a piece of that word out of you and implant it into your wife, just as he did with Elisha, giving him a double portion of Elijah's spirit (2 Kings 2:9-15).

Think of that piece as the seed of the fruit of your tree. With that seed, which carries the life of your tree, God can recreate or multiply you. All He needs is a piece.

> Then He said, "To what shall we liken the Kingdom of God? Or with what parable shall we picture it? It is like a mustard seed which, when it is sown on the ground, is smaller than all the seeds on the earth; But when it is sown, it grows up and becomes greater than all herbs, and shoots out large branches, so that the birds of the air may nest under its shade."
>
> Mk 4:30-32

So, when you look at your wife, understanding that she is a piece of you, it becomes easy for you to follow Eph 5:28, 'so husbands ought to love their own wives as their own bodies; he who loves his wife loves himself', because you realize you have become one flesh (Gen 2:24). It's like Paul states in 1 Thess. 2:8:

> So affectionately longing for you, we were well pleased to impart to you not only the gospel of God, but also our own lives, because you had become dear to us.

God understands if He takes what is precious to you and implants it in your wife, she will become dear to you, causing you to give your very life – your time, your tears, your money – for her and long affectionately for her. However, you will only do that if she is your treasure. Remember that "...where your treasure is, there your heart will be also" (Mt 6:21) and when your heart is with your wife, what is the result?

The heart of her husband safely
trust her; so he will have no lack of gain.

Prov 31:11

Therefore, let wisdom heighten your love.

4. Wisdom helps you recognize your wife.

As you develop in your relationship with wisdom, you will come to know wisdom inside and out. You will know what she likes, what she dislikes, how she speaks, and who she is. You will know her very essence in your spirit so much so that to explain who she really is as a person will leave you at a loss for words.

Because of this relationship, you will not mistake a person of similar characteristics for her. For instance, someone else could look, dress, talk, and move just like wisdom, but instantly you'd know it wasn't her, in much the same way as you'd be able to tell the difference between an impersonator and someone close to you, because of the familiarity you have with them. Likewise, you will have a familiarity with wisdom and that familiarity will help you recognize your wife.

When you recognize your wife, it's not her that you are recognizing, but the wisdom she has become. Remember, wisdom takes care of you according to the specifications of God's purpose for your life. It is a specific wisdom. When you see that wisdom upon a woman, it will be as if you know her. There will be something drawing you to her, a familiarity, a love for her that has been developed in your relationship with wisdom.

This knowledge of wisdom that you will carry around in your spirit will make you so discriminatory that people will think you have impossibly "high standards." It is because when they hear you talk about your desired wife, they will assume it is a list of requirements. However, you are only describing what your spirit sees. Since you won't be able to describe her essence with words, you will begin to talk about how she acts and what she does.

Unfortunately, people are not used to that. They want to hear ten little vague things you desire so they can see how they measure up to your desires, or how they can help find you a wife. However, there is a problem with that.

> The royal daughter is all
> glorious within the palace. Her clothing is woven with
> gold. She shall be brought to the king in robes of many
> colors.
>
> Ps 45:13-14

How can you describe in ten sentences someone who is so intricate... so full of glory...so heavily adorned? It is impossible. Just as a complete description of the Sistine Chapel would be exhaustive, so, too, will be the description of your wife. There will be no other way for you to speak of her essence, except that you speak in the Spirit. Because, again, it is a picture on the inside, a familiarity that will be impossible for you to explain, sensibly, to others.

You could take two wonderful females who are almost indistinguishable from each other in terms of looks, career, or style. Neither has much of an advantage over the other in any area – at least not in the eyes of others. Yet, with your eyes you see one has the essence of the wisdom you've come to know and the other doesn't. So, yes, the other fulfills your ten desires, but she, unlike the first, doesn't have the essence. The essence makes the indistinguishable distinguishable. It really won't matter whether they are 'good girls', or meet the 'requirements'. The only criterion that will matter is the essence.

As a result, you must be careful when describing your desired wife to other females. They may try to become what they can only be if they possess the essence you're looking for, and doing so will cause them to be unrecognizable to the men who are looking for them.

Remember in Genesis, there was nothing Leah could do to make Jacob love her like he loved Rachel, for Leah lacked the essence. So, likewise, you will never truly love a woman who does not possess the essence of the wisdom you've come to know; neither will you be able to give them a clear answer as to why not.

For a long time, I wondered why I could not accurately put into words the essence of that wisdom or the essence of my wife. I found the answer in Prov 19:14.

> Houses and riches are an inheritance from fathers, but a prudent wife is from the Lord.

God wants to make sure you are relying totally on Him. If you were able to describe what you were looking for solely with your intelligence, you would not depend on Him to bring you your wife. However, without Him, you can't describe the essence, the 'it' factor.

Yet, God knows and He is the only one who knows, as He placed the familiarity of that essence in you as a homing device so you'd be able to locate your wife. It is the wisdom in you recognizing the wisdom in her. Because of your relationship with wisdom, your spirit should jump when you see her, just as Elizabeth's womb jumped when she saw Mary.

> Now Mary arose in those days and went into the hill country with haste, to a city in Judah, and entered the house of Zacharias and greeted Elizabeth. And it happened, when Elizabeth heard the greeting of Mary, that the babe leaped in her womb; and Elizabeth was filled with the Holy Spirit. Then she spoke out with a loud voice and said, "Blessed are you among women, and blessed is the fruit of your womb! But why is this granted to me, that the mother of my Lord should come to me? For indeed, as soon as the voice of your greeting sounded in my ears, the babe leaped in my womb for joy. Blessed is she who believed, for there will be a fulfillment of those things which were told her from the Lord."
>
> Lk 1:39-45

As you know, Elizabeth was pregnant with John the Baptist, the one who would prepare the way for Jesus, while Mary was pregnant with Jesus. The interesting thing is Elizabeth's womb jumped when Mary's voice entered her ears, not just because they were in each other's presence. That means Mary's words were saturated by what she was full of on the inside – the life of Jesus, God's salvation.

And, because their purpose was tied to each other (Lk 1:16-17), Elizabeth was able to recognize what Mary was full of with such acuity that it caused her to speak blessings from her spirit concerning Mary, even though Mary had not yet shared with Elizabeth what she was full of.

When you meet your wife, what you are full of will be able to detect what she is full of, because you share the same purpose. That purpose is the thing which ties you together. Again, your wife comes out of you.

> Then the rib which the Lord
> God had taken from man He made into a woman and
> brought her to the man.
>
> Gen 2:22

The word 'made' literally means 'built'. God has taken something from you to build your wife. But, just in case there is confusion, what is God using to build your wife?

> Wisdom has built her house,
> she has hewn out her seven pillars.
>
> Prov 9:1

God is using wisdom to build or construct your wife. Remember, the wisdom you already possess on the inside of you is 'traversing the way of righteousness' (Prov 8:20), which I defined as 'your agreement with God through words, thoughts, and images'. As she moves across your righteousness, she takes the blueprints that have been developed by your words, thoughts, and images and uses them to uses them to build your life, or in this case, your wife. As it states in Is 58:9:

> ...and your righteousness shall
> go before you; the glory of the Lord shall be your
> rear guard.

Your righteousness goes before you to create your life. And the glory of the Lord, or manifestation, is always coming behind you as evidence of what you send out ahead of you. That's how wisdom creates your life, so at every step you see the results of what you've been meditating on.

One suggestion, though. If wisdom is using what's in you to build your wife, make sure the word of God is in your heart in abundance.

> ...for out of the abundance of
> the heart...
>
> Mt 12:34

> ...out of it [the heart] spring
> the issues of life.
>
> Prov 4:23

Keeping your heart full of the word of God concerning a wife gives wisdom the proper material necessary to build your wife – a wife who has spent so much time with wisdom that she has become wisdom and now displays the same characteristics as wisdom.

> The wise woman builds her
> house, but the foolish pulls it down with her hands.
>
> Prov 14:1

Now, just as wisdom has created your life, and gone before you to prepare your wife, your wife, in turn, builds your life using the same wisdom you possess on the inside of you.

> For as woman came from man,
> even so man also comes through woman, but all things
> are from God.
>
> 1 Cor 11:12

> ...a woman shall encompass a man."
>
> Jer. 31:22

Yet, it all starts with wisdom.

Qualifying For A Wife Of Wisdom

Many men may understand finding a wife starts with wisdom. However, not many will qualify for a wife of wisdom because they do not discern the Lord's body (1 Cor 11:29), and they do not develop in the character necessary. You must understand who your future wife is. Look at Prov 24:3-4.

> Through wisdom a house is built, and by understanding it is established; by knowledge the rooms are filled with all precious and pleasant riches.

Out of this scripture, I want to pay particular attention to the word 'house'. In Hebrew, that word is 'bayit (by-yeet)'. It means 'household, family, clan, temple, building, or home'. Through wisdom, your wife is building a household...a family... yet more importantly she has been built as a temple for God.

> Do you not know that you are the temple of God and that the Spirit God dwells in you? If anyone defiles the temple of God, God will destroy him. For the temple of God is holy, which temple you are.
>
> 1 Cor 3:16-17

Now, look at Jhn 14:23

> Jesus answered and said to him, "If anyone loves Me, he will keep My word; and My Father will love him, and We will come and make Our home with him."

And 2 Timothy 2:21

> Therefore, if anyone cleanses himself from the latter, he will be a vessel for honor, sanctified and useful for the Master, prepared for every good work.

When a woman submits herself to wisdom, cleansing herself, and keeping God's Word, Jesus promised to make His home with her and that she would be prepared, or built, for every good work. God also said she would be sanctified, or set apart. Thus, she becomes more than the average woman; she becomes a woman who is sanctified unto God.

So that puts you in an interesting position because if you touch her unworthily, you will suffer the judgment of those who do not discern the Lord's body (1 Cor 11:30).

Do not think for one moment you will be able to ask God for a wife of wisdom, then treat her – the temple of God– any kind of way; not when He promised to destroy those who defile His temple. Nor will God allow just anyone to come to His temple.

Remember, a prudent wife is from the Lord. He is the only one who can give you the highest quality of wife. But, only those who qualify shall receive.

For concerning Jerusalem, the place of His temple, He says:

> Awake, Awake!
> Put on your strength, o Zion;
> Put on your beautiful garments,
> O Jerusalem, the holy city!
> For the *uncircumsized* and the *unclean*
> Shall no longer come to you.'
>
> Is 52:1

Thus says the Lord God: "No
foreigner, uncircumcised in heart or uncircumcised in
flesh, shall enter My sanctuary, including any foreigner
who is among the children of Israel."

Eze 44:9

God is no longer going to allow those whose hearts are not for Him
to enter His temple and cause His covenant to be broken.
He is setting a seal around those women who have cleansed
themselves from all unrighteousness and are now presented as vessels
unto honor. No longer will the uncircumcised in heart, or those
whose hearts are not pure and desiring the things of God, be able to
enter in, even if they are in the church. Because their hearts are not
full of and set on the things of God.
So, who can enter God's temple?

"But the priests, the Levites,
the sons of Zadok, who kept charge of my sanctuary,
when the children of Israel went astray from me, they
shall come near Me to minister to Me; and they shall
stand before Me to offer to Me the fat and the blood,"
says the Lord God. "They shall enter My sanctuary, and
they shall come near My table to minister to Me, and
they shall keep My charge. And it shall be, whenever
they enter the gates of the inner court, that they shall
put on linen garments; no wool shall come upon them
while they minister within the gates of the inner court
or within the house."

Eze 44:15-17

Very simply, those who shall enter in are those whose hearts are for
God, even when everyone else chooses to do things contrary to God's
word. It will be impossible for you to enter into the sanctuary – or
that blessed relationship – and experience its benefits without having
a heart for the things of God. However, when you do, you will be
able to come near His table to minister to Him.

You prepare a table before me
in the presence of my enemies;

Ps 23:5a

...and what is set on your table would be full of richness.

Wisdom has built her house,
She has hewn out her seven pillars;
She has slaughtered her meat,
She has mixed her wine,
She has also furnished her table.
She has sent out her maidens,
She cries out from the highest places of the city.
Whoever is simple, let him turn in here!"

As for him who lacks understanding, she says to him, "Come, eat of my bread and drink of the wine I have mixed. Forsake foolishness and live, and go in the way of understanding."

Prov 9:1-6

When you are at God's table, you are surrounded by richness, understanding and life and are able to overcome the attacks of your enemies.

But, again, it starts with wisdom.

Do Not Release The Seed Before The Time

When God created man, He gave to him seed. His intention was for man to take that seed and plant it in the ground, to take care of it by watering and nourishing it, so that it would grow out of the ground in a physical form called harvest. When that happens, whatever is in that seed has been manifested for all to see – its dimensions, its characteristics, its lifespan, its growth, its role and function here on the earth can now play out before the physical eye.

Thus, at one time, God gave man every kind of seed that was on the earth, knowing that each would produce fruit that yielded more seed. With a seed that produced fruit containing more seed, man was able to grow whatever he desired, agriculturally, without the fear of running out. As long as he continued to farm, the produce of the initial seed would eventually overwhelm his land. Thus, he sowed a seed that produced a fruit that contained 100 seeds, which produced 100 fruit containing 100 seeds, which produced 10,000 fruit, each containing 100 seeds, at which point, growth began to explode exponentially. Since man continued to farm, there was no possibility of a shortage.

So it is with the kingdom of God. Luke 8:11 says:

...The seed is the Word of God.

And v.15 states:

> But the ones that fell on good
> ground are those who, having heard the word with
> a noble and good heart, keep it and bear fruit with
> patience.

God has given us His word as a seed. The Bible contains seed that cover every situation and desire in life, for He gave us '...every herb that yields seed which is on the face of the earth' (Gen 1:29).

When we take the seed of His word that contains the life of what we desire to produce and put it in the ground of our hearts by hearing that word, speaking that word, seeing that word, and pondering that word, we can allow the life of that seed to be seen in our lives. So with a seed and the dominion God has given us, we can change anything through this process, which is called seedtime and harvest.

In the previous chapters, we talked about two preparation principles: saturating your heart with God's specific word for your life and developing a relationship with wisdom. We also briefly discussed the power of an image, particularly how our thoughts shape our lives, and seedtime and harvest. However, if we do not get a hold of this third preparation principle and fully develop it, we can short-circuit our entire system of belief, making everything else we're doing ineffective.

Thus, if one does not effectively operate this third principle, it will be impossible to proficiently develop an image, see yourself in a desired place, change your thoughts, saturate your heart with God's specific word for your life and develop a relationship with wisdom. However, if you grasp this third principle, the efficiency with which you'll bring forth harvest will be phenomenal.

Preparation Principle 3: Do not release the seed before the time.

As I read Prov 5:7-14, I began to notice new meanings I had not fully perceived before. I knew He was imploring us to avoid fornication or sex before marriage because of the terrible effects it brings, but I begin to see the reasons clearly as they pertain to seedtime and harvest. This is the one area where most men fail. We understand that we *shouldn't* fornicate, but we do not understand why not. If we pay close attention to these scriptures, we'll begin to see how fornication derails our efforts to operate in faith.

> Therefore hear me now, my children and do not depart from the words of my mouth. Remove your way far from her, and do not go near the door of her house, lest you give your *honor* to others; and your years to the cruel one; lest aliens be filled with your *wealth*, and your labors go to the house of a foreigner; and you mourn at last, when your flesh and your body are consumed, and say: "How I have hated instruction, and my heart despised correction! I have not obeyed the voice of my teachers, nor inclined my ear to those who instructed me! I was on the verge of total ruin, in the midst of the assembly and congregation."
>
> Prov 5:7-14

1. Fornication forfeits the reasons for which we believe God.

Through fornication, you give you honor to others, your years to the cruel one, aliens are filled with your wealth and your labors go to the house of a foreigner.

What are you giving away when you give your honor to others? In the Hebrew, the word for honor is 'hod'. It means 'vigor, glory, honor, majesty, beauty, grandeur, excellence in form and appearance'.

When you think of 'vigor', I want you to think of 'great energy', and that is what you have given away – your great energy. Not only that, but you've given away that which makes you excellent. Everything you've been working on for years, you've given away and you have not allowed it to benefit you. Therefore, you remain stuck in the same place; not building momentum and failing to progress. Basically, all you've done is taken the seed God has given you, and for years you used that seed to bring forth a harvest of death, instead of the life you were intended to create.

Remember, the Bible says, 'the wages of sin is death...' (Rom 6:23). There is no way we can participate in fornication and produce the life God desires for us to have; not when we take the seed God has given us and use it to participate in sin. As a consequence, the seed that was intended to be used to produce God's life in us is being used to produce death, or Satan's life, in us. Instead of seeing the goodness of God, we see the despair of Satan:

- We live in houses we weren't designed to live in.
- We drive cars we weren't designed to drive.
- We work at jobs we weren't intended to have.
- We're in relationships we weren't designed to be in.

There is hardly anything in our lives designed by God. Hence, most of it has been produced through the harvest of our sin. Therefore, we are frustrated, hurt, and broken.

2. Fornication reduces our strength

> For by means of a harlot, a
> man is reduced to a crust of bread.
>
> Prov 6:26

Because of our consistent sin, we are a shell of ourselves; reduced to a crust of bread; without substance. We want change. We want to progress. We want to build the life God has for us, but we lack the strength to create the life God designed for us. That's why Prov 31:3 implores us:

> Do not give your strength to
> women, nor your ways to that which destroys kings.

The Hebrew word for 'strength' is 'chayil', which is the same word translated as 'wealth' in Prov 5:10. That word means 'strength, power, force, might, valor, substance, wealth, army, valiant, riches, strong, host'.

Looking once more at Prov 5:10, it says, 'aliens are filled with your wealth; your force, power, might, substance, and valor. So, consequently, your labors – all you fasted, prayed, and sowed for – go to the house (temple; body) of a foreigner.

Who are these aliens; these foreigners, or strangers? They are those who are not like us; not comparable, or suitable for us. They are not the places designed by God for us to sow our seed. When we have sown in a place we know won't bring us "Godly fruit," we have no strength or valor.

3. Fornication prevents us from presenting to our wives an individual who is whole.

A man's desire should be to present himself wholly to his future wife, not in part, for it is what she receives from him that allows her to complement him. What she receives is the blueprint and equipment necessary to maximize her potential and his life.

However, when a man gives a piece of himself to a myriad of women through fornication, he doesn't have much left to give his wife. He has been reduced to crust of bread. If a man can only give a piece of himself to his wife, he inhibits her from fully maximizing her potential and his life. Not only has he robbed his wife, but he has robbed himself. The greatest gift a man can give himself is a wife who is fully equipped.

4. Fornication inhibits our relationship with others.

"You also committed harlotry with the Egyptians, your veryfleshly neighbors, and increased your acts of harlotry to provoke Me to anger. Behold, therefore, I stretched out My hand against you, diminished your allotment, and gave you up to the will of those who hate you, the daughters of the Philistines, who are ashamed of your lewd behavior. You also played the harlot with the Assyrians, because you were insatiable; indeed you played the harlot with them and still were not satisfied. Moreover you multiplied your acts of harlotry as far as the land of the trader, Chaldea; and even then you were not satisfied How degenerate is your heart," says the Lord God, "seeing you do all these things, the deeds of a brazen harlot."

Eze 16:26-30

Therefore, Oholibah, thus says the Lord God: 'Behold, I will stir up your lovers against you, from whom you have alienated yourself, and I will bring them against you from every side...'

Eze 23:22

They will deal hatefully with you, take away all you have worked for, and leave you naked and bare. The nakedness of your harlotry shall be uncovered, both your lewdness and your harlotry.

Eze 23:29

In Eze 16, fornication creates such dissatisfaction that those in the text moved from one partner to another with their character degenerating the further along they went. Similarly, we move in and out of relationships only as a means to satisfy our lust. Once we're through with a relationship, we alienate the individuals involved, never building true intimacy. Subsequently, the other individual ends up hurt and we are affected when he or she deals hatefully with us and takes away all we've worked for.

Yet, it goes beyond that, as it extends into God-ordained relationships as well, including friendships. Gen 2:25 says Adam and Eve were both naked, or transparent. As well, they were not ashamed, disappointed, or embarrassed. However, after they sinned in the Garden, Gen 3:7 says:

Then the eyes of both of them were opened, and they knew that they were naked; and they sewed fig leaves together and made themselves coverings.

Their sin affected their openness with one another. So, likewise, we know what we've been doing. In an attempt to cover ourselves, we hide from all the wonderful friendships we have and future friendships we could have, because we are ashamed. Fornication deprives us of standing tall as we were created to do. As a result, we try to deal with our situations alone, which keep us from sharing with others and them from sharing with us. The result is that every joint can't supply as God intended in Eph 4:16, where each person was able to give something to the organization that allowed it and the individuals to be much stronger.

5. Fornication inhibits our relationship with God.

What was Adam and Eve's response to their sin?

> And they heard the sound of the Lord God walking in the garden in the cool of the day, and Adam and his wife hid themselves from the presence of the Lord God among the trees of the garden.
>
> Gen 3:8

Sin causes us to hide from the most wonderful relationship we can have – our relationship with God. Every time we fornicate, that sin brings condemnation, or guilt. We begin to believe we cannot receive from God, or become who He called us to be. However, 'if our heart does not condemn us, we have confidence toward God' (1 Jhn 3:21).

6. Fornication causes us to be cowards.

When condemnation enters into our hearts, we refuse to stand up and take what is rightfully ours, because sin robs a man of the confidence necessary to appropriate the promises of God. 1 Jhn 3:20 reminds us, '...if our heart condemns us, God is greater than our heart.' So, it is not the condemnation of sin that is the problem. The problem is the lack of confidence, for where there is a lack of confidence, unbelief is present and it is unbelief that keeps God from operating in our lives.

Now He did not do many
mighty works there because of their unbelief.

Mt 13:58

7. Fornication causes us to always be learning without progress.

For men will be
lovers of themselves, lovers of money, boasters, proud,
blasphemers, disobedient to parents, unthankful, unholy,
unloving, unforgiving, slanderers, without self-control,
brutal despisers of good, traitors, headstrong, haughty,
lovers of pleasure rather than lovers of God, having
a form of godliness but denying its power. And from
such people turn away! For of this sort are those who
creep into households and make captives of gullible
women loaded down with sins, led away by various
lusts, always learning and never able to come to the
knowledge of the truth. Now as Jannes and Jambres
resisted Moses, so do these also resist the truth: Men
of corrupt minds, disapproved concerning the faith;
but they will progress no further, for their folly will be
manifest to all, as theirs also was.

2 Tim 3:2-9

Contained in this scripture is the malaise of most men: '...*always
learning and never able to come to the knowledge of the truth;'
'...Men of corrupt minds, disapproved concerning the faith.'*
Why?

Because, their minds have convinced them they can 'creep into
households' and sleep with woman after woman and still receive the
results from God they're looking for. They resist doing it God's
way, because they are lovers of themselves; lovers of pleasure rather
than lovers of God. Therefore, just like a bank rejects an application,
their lack of reverence for the seed God has given disapproves or
disqualifies them from receiving the results faith brings.

In 1 Kngs 18:41-42, Elijah hears the sound of the abundance of rain. He is so consumed with rain on the inside that it moves him to release with his mouth what's on the inside of him. He did not have a choice as Matt 12:34 tells us:

> ...out of the abundance of the
> heart the mouth speaks.

The only way you are able to produce results the way Elijah did is to consume yourself with the word of God, which is likened to rain in Is 55:10-11, until you reach the point of overflow, for Ecc 11:3 tells us:

> If the clouds are full of rain,
> they empty themselves upon the earth.

So, if the goal is to fill like a cloud until it can no longer hold the rain, thereby bringing manifestation, then we must guard ourselves against anything that will decrease the capacity of the cloud.

Too many times we are right at the point of overflow when we allow Satan to divert our attention off of the word and onto a female. Once we yield to sin, we have delayed our manifestation. Prov 13:12 tells us·

> Hope deferred makes the heart sick...

This is all Satan cares about. He doesn't mind you getting the word. He doesn't even mind you filling your heart with the word. He just doesn't want you to reach overflow and produce results.

Isn't it amazing? If Satan directly attacks your faith, you beat his head in with the word. You are strong in faith. However, when he switches tactics and appeals to your sexual desire, you willingly let go of your faith. So, until you learn to possess your body in sanctification and honor (1 Thess. 4:4), you will remain stuck in your present state. Furthermore, where before you were able to fool people for a while, the consistent fruitlessness of your life begins to manifest your folly – the constant release of seed, which is a clear violation of God's word.

There must be reverence for the seed. Many of us are not used to seeing our physical seed, or sperm, as containers of what we are full of. Therefore, we do not reverence our physical seed. So, abstaining from sex becomes focused on the denial of gratification instead of the preservation of what is precious to us.

Understand, just like a word spoken to and received by Mary produced in her a physical seed, so a word spoken to and received by you produces in you a physical seed. Furthermore, as the abundance of your heart is released through your words, the abundance of your heart is also released through your sperm and/or physical seed.

Let's explore your physical seed in more detail. A child would be produced if you were to have sexual intercourse with a woman and your sperm made contact with her egg. Every detail of your child's life is wrapped in that sperm or physical seed – your child's hair, eye color, height, weight, physical composition, ability, personality, the cars your child would drive, the houses your child would live in, schools attended, friends, lives your child would touch, jobs your child would hold, etc. Whether you participated in your child's life or not, a lot of your child's physical features, personality traits, strengths, weaknesses and actions would derive from you, because the seed produces after its kind.

An apple tree produces apples because it is full of apples.

A pear tree produces pears because it is full of pears.

A banana tree produces bananas because it is full of bananas.

So, what are you full of?

Promotion?

Deliverance from an addiction?

Healing in your body?

Financial provision?

A debt-free house or car?

A wife?

Yes, it is true. God has given us seed to sow. However, we must understand when and where to sow. Because we are made in His image, let's find out where He sows His seed.

Lk 8:11

> Now the parable is this: The seed is the word of God.

v.15

> But the ones that fell on the
> good ground are those who having heard the word
> with a noble and good heart keep it and bear fruit with
> patience.

God sows His seed into the ground of our hearts. We are His ground. Therefore, we play a pivotal role in this process, but the seed has not any power until it comes into agreement with the soil. How we receive His seed determines what kind of harvest we produce, as *the quality of the soil determines the quality of the harvest.*

In That Land

Likewise, how the ground we sow into receives the seed determines the harvest that is produced. Therefore, we must follow the advice of Jesus in Mt 7:6.

> ...do not give what is holy to
> the dogs; nor cast your pearls before swine, lest they
> trample them under their feet, and turn and tear you
> in pieces.

So, we must be careful not to commit what is precious to us to others who will not value and care for it the same as we do. We must possess a certain amount of selectivity in deciding into which ground to sow our seed. Remember Mk 4? Some seed fell by the wayside, and was consumed by the birds of the air. Some fell on stony ground, failed to develop roots, and consequently did not produce harvest. Meanwhile some seed fell on good ground and produced a thirty, sixty, or hundredfold harvest.

Thus, we should be looking for good ground, or good land, where we can sow our seed. Because, in Gen 12:1-3, God told Abraham to get out of his country, from his family, and from his father's house to "a land I will show you."

God promised Abraham that myriads of things would happen in "that land:"

"I will make you a great nation"... in that land.
"I will bless you"... in that land.
"And I will make your name great"... in that land.
"And you shall be a blessing"... in that land.
"I will bless those who bless you"... in that land.
"And I will curse him who curses you"... in that land.
"And in you all the families of the earth shall be blessed"...
in that land.

When you find "that land" where God has designed for you
to sow your seed, the increase in every area of your life will be
tremendous! However, you've got to have your seed. It would be a
shame to get to that place without your seed, for that land is fertile
and ready to produce manifold blessings in your life.

But, where is this land, this ground to sow into?

A garden enclosed is my sister,
my spouse, a spring shut up, a fountain sealed.

Song 4:12

Your wife is the place where God designed for you to sow your
precious seed; not every little chick you meet, not your longtime
girlfriend, not even self-gratification is acceptable.

God has set up a system of seedtime and harvest. This system
works agriculturally (if you plant a corn seed in the ground, you
receive corn). This system works socially ("Do unto others as you
would have them do unto you" [Lk 6:31; KJV]). This system works
in every area of life – financially, spiritually, physically, sexually,
etc. Likewise, it works in the marriage relationship. For God took
Adam's rib as a seed to make another him, or someone comparable to
him, because the seed always produces after its kind. Everything you
need to know about a man you can tell by looking at his wife.

For man indeed ought not to
cover his head, since he is the the image and glory
[manifested goodness] of God; but woman is the glory
[manifested goodness] of man.

1 Cor 11:7

This is why in Gen 1:28, after creating them male and female, God 'blessed *them* and God said to *them*, "be fruitful and multiply; fill the earth and subdue it; have dominion over the fish of the sea, over the birds of the air, and over every living thing that moves on the ground." Subsequently, in the next verse, He gave them seed.

God's original intent was to speak a word, a purpose, an assignment to man.

> Then the Lord God took the man and put the man in the Garden of Eden to tend and keep it. And the Lord God commanded the man, saying, "of every tree in the garden you may freely eat; but of the tree of the knowledge of good and evil you shall not eat, for in the day that you eat of it you shall surely die."
>
> Gen 2:15-17

Man would take that word and become full of it.

> ...for out of the abundance of the heart the mouth speaks.
>
> Mt 12:34b

And

> A good man out of the good treasure of his heart brings forth good things.
>
> Mt 12: 35a

At the point he becomes full of that word, man brings it before his wife and comes into agreement with her through the sharing of words.

> Can two walk together, unless they are agreed.
>
> Amos 3:3

Once they are in agreement, through sexual intercourse, man begins to sow into his wife what he is full of.

Therefore a man shall leave his
father and mother and be *joined* to his wife and they
shall become *one flesh.*

Gen 2:24

So what happens next?

And He said, "The kingdom of
God is as if a man should scatter seed on the ground,
and should sleep by night and rise by day, and the seed
should sprout and grow, he himself does not know how.
For the earth yields crops by itself: first the blade,
then the head, after that the full grain in the head.
But when the grain ripens, immediately he puts in the
sickle, because the harvest has come."

Mk 4:26-29

Woman takes that seed and begins to work on bringing forth the
harvest of that seed. How she is able to accomplish this no one
knows.

Remember, God gives a man a prudent wife, or a wife of wisdom
and in Prov 8:30, wisdom refers to herself as a master craftsman.
A wife of wisdom was born to create whatever is committed to her;
whether it is the seed of a house, a business, financial increase, or
the answer to a question, she is equipped to create it and bring it
forth. Subsequently, man is able to take that harvest and use it to
minister to God.

Honor [yield to] the Lord with
your possessions, and with the firstfruits of all your
increase; so your barns will be filled with plenty, and
your vats will overflow with new wine.

Prov 3:9-10

God, in turn, takes that offering, multiplies it, and gives it back to
man to repeat the cycle of increase.

Now, when God increases a thing, how does he increase it?

May the Lord
God of your fathers make you a thousand times more
numerous than you are, and bless you as He has
promised you!

Deu 1:11

God has already established that we should receive increase a thousand times above where we presently are. So let's apply this to what we've already learned.

Remember, God will only allow the pure – the uncircumcised in heart – to enter His temple (Eze 44). In Gen 2:22 and Prov 9:1a, God made – or built – a woman using wisdom, because 'wisdom has built her house'. So, the temple, in this case, represents a woman built by the wisdom of God as a dwelling place.

So, what happens when a man, who is pure in heart, enters the temple regularly and enacts God's system of seedtime and harvest?

Eze 47:1-5

Then he brought me back
to the door of the temple; and there was water [the
word] flowing from under the threshold of temple
toward the east, for the front of the temple faced east;
the water was flowing from under the right side of the
temple, south of the altar. He brought me out by way
of the north gate, and led me around on the outside
to the outer gateway that faces east; and there was
water, running out on the right side. And when the
man went out to the east with the line in his hand,
he measured *one thousand* cubits, and he brought me
through the waters; the waters came up to my ankles.
Again he measured *one thousand* and brought me
through the waters; the water came up to my knees.
Again he measured *one thousand*, and it was a river
I could not cross; for the water was too deep, water
in which one must swim, a river that could not be
crossed.

v.9-10

> And it shall be that every living thing that moves, wherever the rivers go, will live. There will be a very great multitude of fish, because these waters go there; for they will be healed, and everything will live wherever the river goes. It shall be that fishermen will stand by it from En Gedi to En Eglaim; they will be places for spreading their nets. Their fish will be of the same kinds as the fish of the Great Sea, exceedingly many.

v.12

> Along the banks of the river, on this side and that, will grow all kinds of trees used for food; their leaves will not wither, and their fruit will not fail. They will bear fruit every month, because their water flows from the sanctuary. Their fruit will be for food, and their leaves for medicine.

Sexual intercourse is God's supernatural level of seedtime and harvest. It carries with it an accelerated pace, where life is increased a thousand times upon a thousand times upon a thousand times.

From this increase, not only is the married couple blessed, but so are others, also, as rivers begin to flow from the temple. As these rivers flow, they bring life and healing to whatever they touch. Also, the influence of these rivers leads to a great harvest for fishermen, or ' fishers of men', because what flows out of this union is preparing the hearts of men to receive the gospel preached to them as the rivers carry them into churches across the globe.

Because of this river, trees – or deeply rooted producers of recurring fruit – grow up along the banks. Their fruit will be for food, or edification. Their leaves used for medicine, or the healing of ailments, whether physical, financial, spiritual, or emotional.

God intended sex to be a method of multiplication in every area of life through unity and transference (transferring the seed into our wives). However, oftentimes, we have allowed Satan to use this process to multiply his agenda.

Understand, just because we are not taking God's word and depositing it into our wives does not mean the system of seedtime and harvest has been shut off. Gal 6:7-8 states:

> Do not be deceived, God is not mocked; for whatever a man sows that he will also reap. For he who sows to the flesh will of the flesh reap corruption, but he who sows to the Spirit will of the Spirit reap everlasting life.

Whatever we sow, if not uprooted, will produce a harvest in our lives. If we sow to the flesh, as Satan would have us do, we shall reap corruption. The Bible says, 'for the wages of the sin is death' (Rom 6:23). Therefore, when we enter into fornication we sow into that woman death, because our actions have separated us from God, since he cannot be a part of sin.

When that seed enters her ground, she produces the harvest, which is death. If the two of you continue to fornicate, the ground that was created to bring forth the life of God's word becomes proficient at producing death, so that nothing in her life works as intended. She becomes unrecognizable to the man who is looking for her, because she is producing fruit of your wicked seed, instead of being fertile ground prepared to produce a harvest of the seed he has to sow. He's looking for a place to sow corn seed and she is producing thorns and thistles, because she, also, is not producing your life, for your righteous seed died the moment you illegally penetrated her garden.

Furthermore, things won't work in your life and you will become a carrier of death, because you continue to eat her fruit (death), which bears seed that produces after its kind. So, because of this, Satan's life is magnified, and the life God has ordained for you is hindered here on earth. This is the reason Satan constantly pushes the agenda of fornication and homosexuality. If Satan convinces people it's okay, he can establish his kingdom here on the earth.

What Satan has done, through pornographic images and lewd words, is turn sex into a mechanism for physical gratification. So, we willingly do whatever is necessary to gratify ourselves. He has, effectively, removed any consideration of what we are sowing. We have failed to look at sex as a creator of our lives, instead viewing it only as an instrument of pleasure.

We have to begin to recalibrate our thinking to see it the way God does. Then, and only then, will we respect sexual intercourse. We must begin to see it as it was seen in the Song of Solomon. In this book of the Bible, Solomon always referred to the physical features of the Shunamite woman, because as a man filled with vision, he was noticing the beauty of his garden and the fruit it produced. He saw the end picture, whereas she constantly referred to his characteristics; as the ground, she saw the elements – the materials – required to create what he saw.

As men, we are visionaries. We develop the image, the blueprint, or the hope of a thing. That's why we have a natural tendency to sleep immediately after sex. At that point, the image of what we are sowing is intended to be brought before the mind's eye.

Remember, God allowed Adam to sleep, or dream. When he awoke, he was presented with Eve. By his response, "This is now bone of my bone and flesh of my flesh; she shall be called woman, because she was taken out of man," we can tell he was not surprised to see her, for she looked exactly like the image he had developed while sleeping.

Once we have developed an image, we have developed hope. Every hope requires faith as the substance necessary to bring it to pass.

> Now faith is the substance of things hoped for, the evidence of things not seen.
>
> Heb 11:1

When we release seed, we are releasing the substance to build what we hope for into our wives, so they will have the material necessary to construct the image we've developed.

So, when we get the word and begin to fill up with it, there is a natural desire to sow, a desire driven by a yearning to fulfill, to "...be fruitful and multiply," (Gen 1:28), establishing God's kingdom on the earth.

This is important to understand as single men in order that we can be vigilant in establishing boundaries that support our decision to exercise abstinence. We must recognize that just as we have a natural desire to sow upon hearing the word of God, so too do females have a natural desire to receive upon hearing the word. And, if we do not establish boundaries, we will continue to allow Sunday to be the day of greatest sin, permitting Satan to snatch the word out of our hearts, because we do not understand how this process operates.

What must we understand?

We must understand what to do with our seed as single men.

Remember, God takes the rib out of man and uses it to create woman. So, the wisdom that is in our future wife to take care of us is the same wisdom we already possess.

Also, the process of building faith as Abraham did by developing the image on the inside through words, thoughts, inner vision, desires, emotions, and actions is called righteousness (Gen 15:5-6; Gen 17:5; heb 11:17-19).

Lastly, remember faith is required as substance to bring our hope, or image, to pass. Now, look, again, at what wisdom says in Prov 8:20-21:

I traverse [walk about] the way
of righteousness, in the midst of the paths of justice,
that I may cause those who love me to inherit wealth,
that I may fill their treasuries.

Wisdom wants to bring about for us, as single men, the same results she would bring for us through our wives. She wants to go back and forth over the righteousness we've developed through our words, thoughts, inner vision, desires, emotions, and actions, so she can bring it to pass in our lives.

But, remember, 'faith is the substance of things hoped for...' (heb 11:1). If we do not keep the seed of faith in us, then wisdom does not have the substance necessary to bring forth our righteousness.

So, as single men, we must keep our seed to supply wisdom with the material to cause us to inherit wealth, and, by keeping that seed, we are proving we love her.

More importantly, we must recognize that keeping our bodies

holy is a commandment of the Word we profess to live by. And Is 1:19 clearly states, 'If you are willing and obedient, you shall eat the good of the land.'

Well, what does the Bible say about sex before marriage?

> Flee sexual immorality. Every sin a man does is outside the body, but he who commits sexual immorality sins against his own body. Or do you not know that your body is the temple of the Holy Spirit who is in you, whom you have from God, and you are not your own? For you were bought at a price; therefore glorify God in your body and in your Spirit, which are God's.
>
> 1 Cor 6:18-20

The Bible makes it very clear. We are to avoid sexual immorality. It's not because God is being mean and restrictive. It's that God understands that through sexual intercourse, seed is released and sown. If you are sowing your seed in places God has not designed for you, you cannot produce the life He has for you. And, again, if you are eating of the fruit of sin, you become a carrier of death. So that leads to the destruction of your own body. God has given 'each seed its own body' (1 Cor 15:38), and when you mishandle the seed, you simultaneously mishandle the body that covers it.

We must begin to look at our bodies – filled with seed – as a tithe unto the Lord. What happens when we begin to take this mindset?

> "Bring all the tithes into the storehouse that there may be food in my house, and try Me now in this," says the Lord of hosts, "If I will not open for you the windows of heaven and pour out for you such blessing that there will not be room enough to receive it. And I will rebuke the devourer for your sakes, so that he will not destroy the fruit of your ground, nor shall the vine fail to bear fruit for you in the field," says the Lord of hosts; "and all nations will call you you blessed, for you will be a delightful land," says the Lord of hosts.
>
> Mal 3:10-12

Therefore, it is vitally important that you 'present your body as a living sacrifice' (Rom 12:1); an offering; a tithe; a dedicated thing. Because, on your wedding night, when you enter the temple (which I liken to your wife), you will go before His table and minister to Him by offering up the dedicated thing. When you do, God will cause a blessing to rest in, and upon, your house. Look at Eze 44:29-30:

> They shall eat the grain offering, the sin offering, and the trespass offering; every dedicated thing in Israel shall be theirs. The best of all firstfruits of any kind, and every sacrifice of any kind from all your sacrifices, shall be the priest's; also you shall give to the priest of the first of your ground meal to cause a blessing to rest [or be secure] on your house.

In that time, the offerings, all firstfruits, every sacrifice, and every dedicated thing belonged to the priest. You would bring it to them so a blessing would rest, or be secure, on your house. Well, today, who is our priest?

> seeing then that we have a great High Priest who has passed through the heavens, Jesus the son of God...
> Heb 4:14

So, we have a High Priest in Jesus, to whom we offer every dedicated thing, which according to 2 Tim 2:21,is those who cleanse themselves from dishonor. Those individuals are vessels 'for honor, sanctified (set apart and dedicated), and useful for the Master.'

Now, here's what's going on.

In classical times, when a man desired to marry a young woman, he would give to her father a payment called a brideprice. Likewise, when we desire to marry one of the Heavenly Father's daughters, we must come with a brideprice. So, as we're storing up seed, we're storing up payment for the greatest gift we can give, which is a man who is whole, possessing seed to sow filled with God's word. And we're also storing up payment for the greatest gift we can receive, because our wives come with a dowry.

A dowry, in classical times, was money, goods, or estate brought to the husband by the woman upon their marriage. It was given to her by her father as an early dispersal of her portion of the family's inheritance. This was done to ensure that the husband would be able to care for the bride in just the same manner as her father would.

So, likewise, when we come with a brideprice, God counters with a dowry, or a blessing, to ensure we are able to care for His daughters in just the same manner as He would.

God gives us an enablement to do whatever is necessary to take care of His daughters, our wives. And, because the Bible says faith is working by love (Gal 5:6), when we devote ourselves to loving our wives, 'as Christ also loved the church and gave Himself for her' (Eph 5:25), we energize her faith, making it much easier for her to receive the seed we sow, crack it open, and bring forth harvest.

God gave us this enablement to take care of her, knowing she, in turn, would take care of us and bring our life forth.

> For as woman came from man,
> even so man also comes through woman, but all things
> are from God.
>
> 1 Cor 11:12

And

> ...A woman shall encompass [cause to come
> about] a man [champion; mighty man].
>
> jer. 31:22b

Look at Song of Solomon 7:10-13:

> I am my beloved's, and his
> desire is toward me. Come, my beloved, let us go forth
> to the field; let us lodge in the villages, let us get up
> early to go to the vineyards; let us see if the vine has
> budded, whether the grape blossoms are open, and the
> pomegranates are in bloom. There I will give you my
> love. The mandrakes give off a pleasant fragrance, and
> at our gates are pleasants fruits, all manner, new and
> old, which I have laid up for you, my love.

Here, the wife is imploring her husband, the man who desires her, to come with her to the field to see what harvest has come forth from the seeds sown. In their garden is new fruit from seed sown while married. But, there is also old fruit, which has been laid up. Where did that old fruit come from?

That old fruit came from the seed you kept, allowing wisdom to traverse it. Now that wisdom is operating through your wife, that which was laid up for you is springing forth through the garden of your wife. Yes, wisdom will bring you harvest as a single man. Yet, there are some things reserved for the harvest of marriage. But, you've got to be willing to pay the brideprice.

Sexual intercourse is well worth the wait, in order to pay the brideprice. After all, you cannot receive the dowry without paying the brideprice. Look at Ex 22:16-17:

> If a man entices a virgin who is
> not betrothed, and lies with her, he shall surely pay the
> brideprice for her to be his wife. If the father refuses
> to give her to him, he shall pay money according to the
> brideprice of virgins.

The father, in this instance, is under no obligation to pay a dowry, which is why many marriages are failing today. There is not any respect for the brideprice. Therefore, God is not under obligation to bless it. However, if there is premarital sex, there is still a brideprice to be paid.

If you've gone around sleeping with woman after woman, thinking it was without payment, the brideprice must still be paid. You did not marry them, but you still must pay for them, as your forfeited harvest went to pay the brideprice.

You must be willing to store up seed to pay the brideprice.

But, what if you've already released the seed?

Joel 2:15-16

> Blow the trumpet in zion,
> consecrate a fast call a sacred assembly; gather the
> people, sanctify the congregation, assemble the elders,
> gather the children and the nursing babes; let the

bridegroom go out of his chambers, and the bride from
her dressing room.

v.18-19

Then the Lord will be zealous
for His land and pity His people. The Lord will answer
and say to His people, "Behold, I will send you grain
and new wine and oil, and you will be satisfied by
them; I will no longer make you a reproach among
the nations."

v.25

"So, I will restore to you the
years that the swarming locust has eaten, the crawling
locust, the consuming locust, and the chewing locust,
My great army which I sent among you."

Repent and live a consecrated life and the restoration of God
will bring forth newness of life. All of your sins shall be washed
away.

So, let's continue to prepare and progress.

Developing Godly Friendships

In the previous chapters, we've talked about preparing ourselves for the wives God has for us. We've discussed the importance of saturating ourselves with the specific word of God for our lives. We've discussed developing a relationship with wisdom. As well, we've learned the importance of not releasing the seed before the time.

Now I would like to mention some things we can do to position ourselves to receive the wife God has for us. It is one thing to be prepared for a wife, but we also need to be in the proper position to receive her.

The very first thing I believe is necessary to positioning yourself for a Godly wife is the development of Godly friendships with both males and females. I believe it is important for you to surround yourself with people who will build you up and develop your character. Prov 27:17 states:

> As iron sharpens iron, so man
> sharpens the countenance of his friend.

What are some things I can learn from developing Godly relationships with other males?

Well, first and foremost, there is the strengthening of character mentioned in Prov 27:17. Whatever area you find yourself weak in, they are able to strengthen. Perhaps you didn't grow up understanding how to establish a budget. Through a relationship with someone who has, you can strengthen an area of weakness, and that will further prepare you for your wife.

Maybe you need the experience of someone who has been where you are and successfully gone through the challenge you are dealing with now. It brings great comfort to know that your situation is not unique, that others have triumphed in that area. After all, 'no temptation has overtaken you except such as is common to man' (1 Cor 10:13)

Perhaps, it's the safety of having a multitude of counselors that you need (Prov 11:14). Having friends who can correct you when you're wrong, provide direction when you're lost, encourage you when you're down, pour out the love of God upon you, cover you with prayer, and hear God on your behalf is vital. Sometimes it takes someone with a fresh set of eyes and ears to guard us from getting off track.

Remember, whatever God is going to do in your life, He will always do through an individual. Yes, God can use a complete stranger, but it is much easier for Him to move in your life when you open yourself to the friendship of others. After all, people who know and love you are much more likely to be moved with compassion on your behalf because they already know you.

The one key to keep in mind as you move to establish these Godly friendships is to surround yourself with men who are as you desire to be. It is not a selfish thing to change your environment upward, because after you have completed your transition, you will reach back and mentor someone else, while also reaching ahead to someone further along than you.

The mistake many men make when trying to grow and change is trying to grow and change within the same environment. They lack mentors. Therefore, they fail when they could have had an easier road of success by following the blazed trail of someone else.

If you have this picture of this awesome wife, then you're going to have to push upward in your relationships, because the wife you're looking for is going to be looking for someone as you desire to be.

Think of it this way. There is a woman who is everything you desire in a wife, and she is looking to marry a politician. Fortunately, for you, by calling you are a politician. Now you must decide how to meet this woman. Would you have the greatest probability of success by hanging around musicians and artists? Or, would you have the greatest probability of success by surrounding yourselves with other politicians, going where they go, and doing what they do?

This is the choice you must make. You must choose to be around the people who are as you are called. The wife you desire is not among the artists and musicians. She is among the circle of politicians. Now, through the relationships of those like you, you are able to meet your wife, because she may very well find your friend first, who introduces the two of you to each other.

Hanging around the environment of those who are called as you are called allows you to become comfortable in that environment, so that you are able to display confidence and ease when you meet a potential wife. If you do not spend time in that environment, you will appear as if you do not belong there, even though you are one of them.

This is one of the reasons why I feel it is also necessary to establish Godly friendships with females who are like what you desire. You become comfortable communicating with that type of female. But also:

1. Birds of a feather flock together. A friend will be able to introduce you to someone of the same circle.

2. You learn what is required to love your future wife by listening to what your friends have to say.

3. You learn to see females as members of the body of Christ, not as sexual objects and not as adversaries.

4. They became the example by which you are able to effectively qualify potential spouses.

5. They may be able to see things in our potential wives that males won't, because they think differently.

Remember, relationships are very important in the kingdom of God. If He is going to do anything in your life, it's going to be through the avenue of another individual. Who you allow yourself to be hooked up to in friendship will either enable or inhibit what God is trying to do in your life. Make the decision to stay in the right circle.

Living As You Were Called

God has prepared, and made ready, the good life for you to live. The question that enters most minds is, what is the good life and how do I enjoy it?

Most of what I learned in answering this question came from three places. The first was a teaching done by a minister named Michael Smith, who used to be an associate minister at World Changers. The early portion of this chapter is largely attributed to his teaching on portion.

The other places where I learned about living the good life and living as you were called came from studying the lives of Esau and Jacob, as well as the journey of Jonah.

So when we talk about the good life, what are we talking about? We are talking about that which is God-breathed to you. That is the thing God has designed specifically for you. From this point on, we'll refer to it as 'portion'. According to Minister Smith, portion is the pre-allocation of God's goodness tailor-made for your life.

God's portion for your life is not something that is man-reasoned. It is divinely inspired by God, tailor-made to the way you are wired.

Therefore, if it is not suited to your desires, or your tastes, that can't be God. It is not His method of operation to bring things into your life that do not synchronize with your uniqueness.

The challenge that most people face is determining whether a thing is God-breathed for their life or man-reasoned. When you can't tell the difference, you begin to step outside the portion for your life, where life just isn't as good, because all God has for you resides inside your portion.

This has happened to me plenty of times. I would see what someone else was doing, successfully, and decide to pursue it as well, only to fail where they had success, because it was not my portion. Therefore, I found myself pursuing something that was intentionally being kept away from me. Until I found and resided in my portion, I could not enjoy success. When I learned to stay in my portion and to maximize it, I begin to enjoy life, and remained free from desiring someone else's portion.

Understand that what God has for you belongs to you. What He has for me belongs to me. And with that understanding, we can rejoice in what is ours. It does not matter if your home is bigger than mine – or smaller – I will rejoice with you, anyway, because it's what God has for you, not me.

He has a home for me, cars for me, a wife for me, a career and ministry for me; and it's all, specifically, designed for me. Therefore, I don't have to concern myself with yours, because I am thoroughly pleased with mine.

I cannot allow myself to be distracted by what someone else has; doing so will cause me to be discontent with the portion God has given me. Therefore, I must avoid the wandering eye and the wandering ear, and refuse to allow what I see and hear to cause me to lose focus. And I must follow col. 3:2: 'set your mind on things above, not on things on the earth.'

But how does one enjoy their portion in life?

1. Portion is enjoyed when you're thankful.

You have to reach a point where you understand that the things in your life, now, are there for you to enjoy, whether it is a little or a lot. Maybe God didn't call you to be a lead singer, but be thankful He called you to sing.

2. Portion is maintained when you are humble.

At this stage, you are no longer comparing yourself to anyone else. Your sole focus is on what is God-breathed to you. If your portion is larger than someone else's you don't gloat in it. If your portion is smaller than someone else's, you aren't jealous or feeling inferior. You have your portion, they have theirs, and yours is all you're concerned about.

3. It is expanded when you're faithful.

What does Luke 16:10 say?

> He who is faithful in what is
> least is faithful also in much; and he who is unjust in
> what is least is unjust also in what is much.

You must be faithful over the small bit of your portion God has already poured out, in order for you to receive more. You're asking Him for more, and He wants to give it to you. However, He can only do so when you are maximizing the amount of your portion presently possessed, without trying to cross the boundaries of someone else's portion.

When you stay inside your portion, you will discover life speeds up. God recognizes that you are ready to do His will for your life and live as you were called; therefore He begins to fast track your travels like he did with Jonah.

In the book of Jonah, we find God issuing a call – a portion – out to Jonah. Yet Jonah chose to go on His own journey, only to discover he could not escape the bounds of God's portion for his life. Jonah thought he could make his way prosperous elsewhere, only to discover that that which is God-breathed will always prevail over what is man-reasoned.

Jonah 1:1-4

> Now the word of the Lord
> came to Jonah the son of Amittai, saying, "Arise, go to
> Nineveh, that great city, and cry out against it; for their
> wickedness has come up before me." But Jonah arose
> to flee to Tarshish from the presence of the Lord. He

went down to Joppa, and found a ship going to Tarshish;
So he paid the fare, and went down into it, to go with
them to Tarshish from the presence of the Lord. But
the Lord sent out a great wind on the sea, and there
was a mighty tempest on the sea, so that the ship was
about to be broken up.

v.15
So they picked up Jonah and
threw him into the sea, and the sea ceased from its
raging.

Jonah thought he would be able to escape God's will, and many
of us are like that.   But, God always knows how to capture the
attention of men.   Because of his disobedience, Jonah was forced to
spend three days and three nights in the belly of a fish.   Only after
his repentance was he able to escape. Watch what happened.

Jonah 2:10
So the Lord spoke to the fish,
and it vomited Jonah onto dry land.

Jonah 3:1-14
Now the word of the Lord
came to Jonah the second time, saying, "Arise, go to
Nineveh, that great city, and preach to it the message
that I tell you." So Jonah arose and went to Nineveh,
according to the word of the Lord. Now Nineveh
was an exceedingly great city, a three day journey in
extent. And Jonah began to enter the city on the first
day's walk...

Once Jonah decided to reside in his portion, living as he was
called, things begin to happen at an accelerated pace.   Instead of
being spat out in the middle of the ocean, God caused the fish to
spit him out on dry ground, and a three-day journey took Jonah one
day.   Being in his portion caused what should have been long and
arduous to be short and simple.

What God designed for you can only be enjoyed inside portion

God had a word for Nineveh, to be delivered by Jonah. Upon hearing the words spoken by Jonah, Nineveh repented, so the prophecy did not come to pass. This turn of events had Jonah so distraught he wanted to die. But God spoke to him in Jonah 4:11

> And should I not pity
> Nineveh, that great city, in which are more than one
> hundred and twenty thousand persons who cannot
> discern between their right hand and their left – and
> much livestock.

What was God saying to Jonah?

He was trying to reveal to Jonah the expansion of his portion. After all, here is this great city that has just repented before God. Yet, they did not know which way to go. Who would lead them? Jonah!

Furthermore, God reveals to Jonah there is much livestock in the land, indicating great wealth. All that Jonah was looking for was in his portion in Nineveh, because God knew they would honor Jonah by bringing him substance as he instructed them in how to live. What God had for Jonah could not be enjoyed until Jonah resided inside his portion. So it is with us. To experience what God has, we must live as we were called.

In order to obtain the wife you're looking for, you must stay inside of your portion and live as you were called. Look at Esau and Jacob. One decided to live inside of his portion; the other chose not to. Look at Rom 9:12-13

> It was said to her, "the older
> shall serve the younger." As it is written, "Jacob, I
> have loved, but Esau I have hated."

Here we see God loved, or accepted, Jacob. But He hated, or rejected, Esau. What was it about Esau that caused God to reject him?

Now Jacob cooked a stew; and
Esau came in from the field, and he was weary. And
Esau said to Jacob, "Please feed me with that same
red stew, for I am weary." Therefore his name was
called Edom [red]. But Jacob said, "Sell me your
birth-right as of this day." And Esau said, "Look, I am
about to die; so what is this birthright to me?" Then
Jacob said, "Swear to me as of this day." So he swore
to him, and sold his birth-right to Jacob. And Jacob
gave Esau bread and stew of lentils; then he ate and
drank, arose, and went his way. Thus Esau *despised*
his birthright.

Gen 25:29-34

God rejected Esau, because Esau despised, or counted as nothing, the birthright. The birthright entitled Esau to headship of the family and a double share of the family's inheritance. However, Esau was not concerned about the birthright. His eye was on the blessing, which was given to the eldest son from the father as a way of transferring the family's material property, aspirations, and spiritual promises. The blessing carried three important elements: material property; political supremacy; and a cursing of all enemies. That was Esau's downfall. He thought he could get the blessing, or the empowerment, to carry out the position, without operating in the position (birthright). Esau's heart was not for God, because Esau did not want to operate in the position – the call – God had placed on his family. He just wanted the status, the power, and the substance that was given to carry out the position. This is evident, because Esau refused to live as he was called.

Gen 25:27

So the boys grew. And Esau
was a skillful hunter, a man of the field; but Jacob was
a mild [complete] man, dwelling in tents.

Esau was a hunter, but Abraham and Isaac were shepherds. Instead of operating like them, Esau was out in the fields doing his own thing. Meanwhile, Jacob was a 'complete' man, learning how to run the entire affairs of the estate. Jacob spent more time preparing for the position as head of the family than Esau, because Esau did not intend to operate in the position. He just assumed he would get the perks and leave the responsibility of the position to Jacob.

So when Jacob, who has been preparing and looking for an opportunity to supplant (take the place of) Esau, asks him to sell him his birthright, Esau readily does so, because it is a position he never intends to fulfill. However, Esau's thinking is flawed, because Esau's heart is not for God. Esau doesn't understand he is weary because he is out of position, as weariness is a sign of being in a place God has not designed for you. Look at these scriptures.

> Have you not known?
> Have you not heard?
> The everlasting God, the land,
> The Creator of the ends of the earth,
> Neither faints nor is weary
> His understanding is unsearchable.
> He gives power to the weak, and to
> those who have no might He increases strength.
> Even the youths shall faint and be weary, and
> the young men shall utterly fall. But those who
> wait [serve] on the Lord shall renew their strength;
> they shall mount up on wings like eagles, they shall
> run and not be weary, they shall walk and not
> faint.
>
> Is 40:28-31

> Come to Me, all you who labor
> and are heavy laden, and I will give you rest. Take
> My yoke upon you learn from Me, for I am gentle and
> lowly in heart, and you will find rest for your souls. For
> my yoke is easy and my burden is light.
>
> Mt 11:28-30

Also, Esau, doesn't understand that he doesn't have to go to another man for provision. Deu 8:3 says, "Man shall not live by bread alone; but man lives by every word that proceeds from the mouth of the Lord." He did not recognize that the birthright and the blessing are bestowed through the avenue of words. Therefore, all of his needs would have been met if he had gotten inside the position. If Esau had understood this, his response would not have been, "So what is this birthright to me?" The birthright is everything. Everything you need is in the birthright: the position; the portion; the call of God for your life. That's why God does not want you to be like Esau.

> lest there be any fornicator
> or profane [godless] person like Esau, who for one
> morsel of food sold his birthright. For you know that
> afterward, when he wanted to inherit the blessing, he
> was rejected, for he found no place for repentance,
> though he sought it diligently with tears.
> Heb 12:16-17

Though we do not see him commit such an act, Esau is likened by God to a fornicator. When you choose to commit fornication with another individual, you are going to them to eat of their bread, the substance they have. It's what the harlot spoke of in Prov 9:17, "Stolen water is sweet, and bread eaten in secret is pleasant." When you do so instead of eating the bread of wisdom (Prov 9:5), you are reduced to a crust of bread (Prov 6:26). You have become like Esau.

Fortunately, for us, unlike Esau, we have redemption in Christ Jesus (rom 3:24). However, if we choose to live outside of our portion, doing our own will, and seeking others for our provision, then we will always be stuck in a cycle of weariness and tears, as we cry out to God for the blessing, while ignoring the birthright.

Jacob didn't ignore the birthright. He asked Esau for the birthright without asking for the blessing. Esau would not have given up the blessing if asked. However, Esau willingly gave up the birthright, or position, for a morsel of food, temporary gratification. That's the same thing we do. Not many of us would give up the blessing if asked. But, for temporary gratification, we step out of position. Why?

Because the blessing always follows the birthright. If we take off the birthright, we take off the blessings. If we put on the birthright, we put on the blessing. That's why Jacob didn't have to ask Esau for his blessing. All he had to do was to obtain the birthright. Once

Esau willingly sold his birthright, the blessing automatically became Jacob's. It did not matter how he obtained it.

> for the children not yet being
> born, nor having done any good or evil, that the purpose
> of God according to election might stand, not of works
> but of Him who calls.
>
> Rom 9:11

Jacob got inside that purpose that was given before they did any good or evil. Therefore, his deceitfulness in obtaining the blessing (Gen 27) could not disqualify him from operating in that blessing. Because he chose to step into the birthright – his position, his portion – his character flaws were covered. And, because Jacob stayed in his portion through all trials – the flight from Esau (Gen 27), the deception of his father-in-law (Gen 29), the flight from his father-in-law (Gen 31) – his portion corrected his character flaws (Gen 32:22-32). Because, through it all, Jacob remained a shepherd.

So what was the result of these two men's lives concerning a wife? Well, Esau married a woman named Mahalath, the daughter of Ishmael, whose name meant 'sickness'. Jacob, on the other hand, was blessed with Rachel as a wife. Her name meant 'ewe, sheep', and she was called to the purpose, as she, herself, was a shepherdess. The question is: What would have happened if Esau had lived as he was called?

Be A Cheerful Giver

What happens when you've tried everything I describe in this book and you still feel that something's missing? You may be having trouble controlling your thoughts, or controlling your flesh, or developing a relationship with wisdom or friendships with others. Maybe none of those are issues for you at all. Maybe you've successfully done all described and now you just need to know how to get the manifestation to break forth. Well, I have the answer.

Be a cheerful giver.

The Bible tells us in 2 Corinthians 9:7 that 'God loves a cheerful giver'. The word for cheerful in Greek is 'hilaros'. This word describes someone who is ready and willing to give without restraint and without being coaxed, to give of generous freewill and with delight.

What happens when we give like this?

> And God is able to make all grace abound toward you, that you, always having all sufficiency in all things, may have an abundance for every good work.
>
> 2 Cor 9:8

God's grace, or His underserved blessing, unmerited favor, *His willingness to get involved in our affairs with His affectionate regard*, is made to abound [have in excess] toward us so that we have an abundance of *whatever* is needed for every good work.

What is it that you need in order to be successful in obtaining a wife? Do you need confidence, joy, peace, self-control, financial stability, friends, favor, the right words, wisdom? God has promised to get involved in whatever way you need Him, so give to Him cheerfully. Keep in mind, though, that if you only give a little, you will only reap a little. If you give bountifully, you will reap bountifully (2 Cor 9:6).

Now, this sounds like I am trying to buy a wife from God or bribe Him. Why am I dealing with money, and how does it relate to the issue of finding a wife?

The reason I'm addressing the issue of money is that Ecc 7:12 informs us that just as wisdom is a defense, so is money. Now this makes sense in the external world. Think for a moment: you may not have the answer to a particular problem, but if you have money, you're able to purchase the expertise of someone who does have the answer you need.

If you read Mt 6:21 and Lk 16:13, you will understand that wherever your treasure is, there is your heart. So when you are truly serving God, you're also serving Him with your money. Your financial gifts to God are proof of your love for Him and your love for Him causes Him to move on your behalf. It is an added benefit that He is all-knowing and all-powerful.

With that in mind, I want to look at some ways that being a cheerful giver can be of benefit to you.

1. Giving breaks the chains of bondage in your life.

No matter what you may be going through, your consistent, cheerful financial gifts cause spiritual power to be released, which breaks the bondage of addiction, negativity, and other strongholds in your life.

> For the weapons of our warfare
> are not carnal but mighty in God for pulling down
> strongholds, casting down arguments and every high
> thing that exalts itself against the knowledge of God,
> bringing every thought into captivity to the obedience
> of Christ.
>
> 2 Cor 10:4 -5

I never noticed until it was pointed out by Bishop Eddie Long that this scripture is actually a continuation of Paul's thoughts concerning giving in 2 Corinthians 9. Paul was trying to tell us that we can give our way out of addiction, out of depression, out of fear, out of any other bondage we're dealing with. By our giving, we release the power of God that breaks the stronghold of negative thoughts and images that cause us to deal with so much mess in our day-to-day lives. Cheerful giving helps us control our mental life so that we think, imagine, and speak in line with God's Word, which of course will eventually cause us to act in line with God's Word.

2. Giving moves God to appear, change who we are, and show us what to do.

Perhaps you've always struggled with your confidence: never thought you were good with women or thought they would like you. Perhaps you're just the opposite: never thought you could be faithful to one woman – just a dog, you are. In either case, you don't have to remain that way, because when you cheerfully give to God, your giving causes Him to want fellowship with you. And when God wants fellowship, His love always compels Him to see what He can do for you. When He asks, tell Him what you desire and He'll bring about that change.

This is nothing new. It happened for Solomon as well as for Saul. In 1 Kings 3, Solomon gave a huge sacrificial offering unto God. That very night, God showed up and asked Solomon what he desired. Solomon responded with a request for wisdom. God honored that request so that a man who did not know what to do became known as the wisest man throughout all lands.

In Saul's case, he made it known in 1 Samuel 9 that he specifically gave money to the man of God 'to tell us our way'. The end result was Saul being turned into another man in verse 6 of 1 Samuel 10.

Saul tapped into a very important idea – sowing into the man of God. Many times we go to church, hear wonderful messages that impart powerful truths into our lives that inspire us to live fuller lives. However, we fail to give back into that minister's life as Gal 6:6 exhorts us to do. When we fail to give back, we are sowing to the flesh, because we are receiving yet not giving in return. That situation is similar to someone sharing of their precious things with you while you keep all of your stuff for yourself. You are hoarding for yourself and that is a greedy, selfish, fleshy act. What you will reap is corruption, because that is what you have sown.

The way we should respond is by giving in return every time someone sows into our lives spiritual blessings. When we do, we have sown to the Spirit – given back, so that the message we heard is able to be preached to others as well – and of the Spirit we shall reap everlasting life. The key to this principle is not growing weary while doing good. At every opportunity, give to those who have shared with you spiritual things. If you never let a moment pass without doing good, you will reap in due season (Gal 6:6-10). This kind of consistent giving will produce tremendous changes in your life that will support your efforts to receive the wife God has for you.

3. Giving causes it to rain in your life.

Do you remember when I said the goal was to fill up like a cloud and produce rain? Remember, the goal should be to be so full of the word of God concerning a wife that you can't help but bring forth manifestation (Ecc 11:3). Well, what happens when you're so full of it that you feel as if you're about to burst at the seams, yet you can't seem to get that cloud to burst and produce rain or manifestation (which in this case is your wife)? Should this happen, give and give big!

In 1 Kngs 18, Elijah the prophet was dealing with a similar situation. There was a drought in the land because Elijah declared there would be no rain except at his word (1 Kngs 17:1). In order to get it to rain three years later, Elijah first poured out three offerings of four waterpots on an altar to God. That very same day, Elijah was found declaring he could hear the sound of abundance of rain (1 Kngs 18:41). After his prayer, it immediately began to rain.

What brought about the rain in Elijah's life?

His willingness to give big!

Remember, when you feel stuck and in need of that breakthrough, give!

4. Giving attracts to you God-ordained relationships.

In the book of Acts, there was a man named Cornelius of whom the Bible said 'he gave alms (financial gifts) generously to the people and prayed to God always' (Acts 10:2).

In return for his generous gifts, God sent unto him Peter, who preached the Gospel to him and his entire household with the results that Cornelius and his household were saved and filled with the Holy Spirit (Acts 10).

What was the reason for this divine relationship?

> ...Your prayers and your alms
> have come up as a memorial before God.
>
> Acts 10:4b

Because of his giving, God brought into Cornelius' life a relationship that changed not only his life, but the lives of his entire household. So does God want to do with you, bringing you divine connections: people who change your life. And the most important relationship he wants to bless you with is a prudent wife. However, you must be willing to give generously and consistently.

Giving is a powerful force when used in conjunction with the other principles I have shared with you. If you try to give without adding to it the other biblical principles, it will do you not a bit of good. You will waste your money. However, used correctly, it can be the dynamite to the rest of your faith, because giving will 'increase the fruits of your *righteousness*' (2 Cor 9:10).

Eight Keys To Recognizing Your Wife

Everything we've talked about in this book has been designed to bring you to the point where you are ready to actively pursue a wife.

In your pursuit, there will be plenty of women who will appeal to you, and you will find yourself asking, "Lord, is this my wife?"

To answer this question, God has given me eight questions I must ask when faced with this question. If I can answer all eight questions in the affirmative, then the answer will be "yes."

Question #1: Does she increase your faithfulness towards God?

> She also lies in wait as for a
> victim and increases the unfaithful among men.
> Prov 23:28

If a harlot increases the unfaithful among men, I believe it is safe to conclude that the wife God has for you should do the opposite and push you toward faithfulness. Judge for yourself the situation. Are you more faithful to the assignments God has given you? Or, are you doing less of what you know you should be doing for God?

You used to go to church three times a week.
You used to pray faithfully every morning.
You used to be busy about the things of God.
How about now?

If you can trace your slackness to your involvement with a particular female, maybe she is not the one for you, because she is causing you to compromise your walk with God. And, what you are willing to compromise in order to keep, you will eventually lose anyway.

However, if this young lady moves you toward faithfulness, so that you are doing, on a more consistent basis, the things instructed of you by God, move on to the next question.

Question #2: Does she nourish your spirit and soul?

You need to have someone in your life that can edify you. As you're busy doing the work God has for you, you may find yourself getting low in the word. It is vitally important to have a spouse who knows how to build you up with the word of God and speak words of affection that build your confidence and self-esteem. That keeps you from falling prey to the traps and attacks of the enemy. Take a look at these scriptures.

> Listen, for I will speak of excellent things, and from the opening of my lips will come right things.
>
> Prov 8:6

> Come, eat of my bread and drink of the wine I have mixed.
>
> Prov 9:5

> Let my beloved come to his garden and eat its pleasant fruits.
>
> Song 4:16b

In determining whether or not she nourishes your spirit and soul, pay very close attention to the words that come out of her mouth, because her mouth will reveal what's in her heart. Pay attention to what she consumes through books, music, television, and other sources, because that's what she's feeding her heart. So, consequently, that's what she's going to feed you.

You need a woman who knows the word, eats the word, lives the word, and speaks the word. You need a woman who knows how to fall on her knees and pray for you, watching over you with the dominion given to her by God. You need a woman who knows she is in God, because if she doesn't, her feast isn't complete. And when you sit down at her table to eat what she has prepared, something will be lacking. As a result, you will walk away from her presence malnourished.

You need a woman who knows when and how to stroke your ego. This world may try to beat you down, but if you can just get in her presence, or hear her voice, she'll make you feel like a king. That's why Prov 8:15 says:

> By me kings reign.

Why?

Because she knows how to build you up. Therefore, 'her husband is known among the gates' (Prov 31:23).

Question #3: Does she bring increase into your life?

> I traverse the way of righteousness, in the midst of the paths of justice, that I may cause those who love me to inherit wealth that I may fill their treasuries.
>
> Prov 8:20-21

> He who finds a wife finds a good thing, and obtains favor from the Lord.
>
> Prov 18:22

When you find a wife of wisdom, there should be increase in your life. Are things increasing since she has come into your life? Or, are they decreasing?

God is a God of increase. In Deu 1:11, He promises to increase you a thousand times more than you are. There isn't any possible way God would bring you a wife who would not bring increase into your life. Your life should explode because of her involvement in it.

Question #4: Do you naturally give yourself for her like Christ gives Himself for the church?

> Husbands, love your wives, just as Christ also loved the church gave Himself for her, that He might sanctify, and cleanse her with the washing of water by the word, that He might present her to Himself a glorious church, not having spot or wrinkle or any such thing, but that she should be holy and without blemish. So husbands ought to love their own wives as their own bodies; he who loves his wife loves himself. For no one ever hated his own flesh, but nourishes and cherishes it, just as the Lord does the church.
>
> Eph 5:25-29

Here in this scripture is the most important key to determining if she is your wife – do you naturally give yourself for her like Christ gives Himself for the church? Do you love her like you love yourself?

Many times men say, "if you can find a woman who is with you when you don't have anything, you've got a good woman." That may very well be true. However, it causes us to conduct our search for a wife with a selfish mind-frame. We begin to look for women who love us and treat us well, without proper consideration of how we treat them.

God spoke to my heart one day of finding a wife to love with all my heart. Before I even start to move down the checklist, the primary indicator of my wife is my love for her.

Now, God is not talking about a fleshly love, but a love that causes me to put her interests and needs ahead of mine; a love that will not allow my starving body to eat until she has; a love that will cause me to carry triple the burden, if it eases hers;

a love that doesn't see her as a sexual object, but is fulfilled with just her touch, her presence, her words. This is the love God is talking about, His love that causes you to pour out your life for her, determining to care for her every need. When you find a woman you love like this, 75% of the search is over. Now, you're just making sure the other 25% lines up.

Understand, a relationship does not reach its full potential until the man is consumed by love and is initiating the romance. That makes the woman feel so special that she will do whatever is necessary to help that man fulfill his dream. She will walk through two deserts and the cold night of winter if it means returning his love. And, if you think you can love, wait until you see the love of a woman, who is multiplying the seed of all-consumed love sown into her. But, first you have to find someone you love and naturally give yourself for her like Christ gives Himself for the church.

Question #5: Do you feel safe and secure with her? How easy is it for you to open up to her and trust her?

And they were both naked, the man and his wife, and were not ashamed.

Gen 2:25

For the heart of her husband safely trusts her; so he will have no lack of gain. She does him good and not evil all the days of her life.

Prov 31:11-12

I once asked a co-worker what made him such a good salesman. At the time, he could not answer the question. However, the next day he let me know that the reason he was able to be successful was the assurance that his wife was taking care of things at home. That assurance freed his mind to concentrate on the tasks he had before him, and it motivated him.

Applied to your search, this assurance is what you're looking for. You want someone who is dependable, someone who is considerate of you, someone who will hold your heart safely in her hands.

You're not looking for someone who expresses tremendous amounts of affection, yet disappears from time to time. There should not be any questions, or doubts, about her love and commitment towards you. Because when she is committed to you, you'll find it much easier to open up to her concerning your heart.

However, being transparent with a woman is also a function of your love for her and your personal development. If you truly love her, your love naturally expresses itself through opening up and sharing with her.

The other factor is your personal development. By that, I mean do you have trust issues? If all the other questions are answered in the affirmative, take a close look at yourself and make sure there is not something in you that's keeping you from expressing true intimacy.

Question #6: What is the witness of the Holy Spirit and your initial reaction?

Most people do not believe in love at first sight. And for the most part, neither do I. What I do believe is that God makes presentations, and when He makes a presentation, there is something about that person that hooks in your soul.

Now, that presentation may not be the first time you lay eyes on her. But, at that moment, it's as if you're seeing her for the first time.

This step is the hardest for me to explain, because I do not want to be accused of saying it should be love at first sight. I'm not. I just don't believe it takes all day to determine whether or not we feel someone has the potential to be what we are looking for in a wife. I think if most men are honest with themselves, then they know if there is true, genuine attraction that is causing them to say, "Oh!"

You may not know if the relationship is going to work, but you definitely know if she's 'it' for you or not. I think if we pay more attention to that initial reaction, we will have less failure and less baggage. I believe that positive initial reaction is part of the witness of the Holy Spirit.

When you wait for that positive initial reaction and the witness of the Holy Spirit, you don't ever have to worry about ending up with someone who is not what you like. She may not be exactly what you thought you liked, but, when you allow God to direct you, there's no need to worry about receiving a spouse you aren't thoroughly pleased with. And it is clear to me that it doesn't have to take all day.

> Then the rib
> which the Lord God had taken from man He made into
> a woman, and He brought her to the man, and Adam
> said, "This is bone of my bones and flesh of my flesh;
> she shall be called woman, because she was taken out
> of man."
>
> Gen 2:22-23

Notice, Adam instantly recognized her as a presentation from God, and immediately took her as his wife.

> Then Isaac brought her into
> his mother Sarah's tent; and he took Rebekah and
> she became his wife, and he loved her. So Isaac was
> comforted after his mother's death.
>
> Gen 24:67

Isaac had just met Rebekah for the first time. Yet he, too, instantly recognized her and loved her. It didn't take him long.

> Now Jacob loved Rachel; so
> he said, "I will serve you seven years for Rachel your
> younger daughter."
>
> Gen 29:18

Jacob had only known Rachel for one month when he made this proposal to Laban. Yet, he was so convinced that he agreed to work seven years for her, though it ended up being twenty-one.

> You have ravished
> my heart, my sister, my spouse; You have ravished my
> heart with one look of your eyes with one link of your
> necklace.
>
> Song 4:9

It doesn't take all day. So, pay attention to the witness of the Holy Spirit and your initial reaction.

Question #7: How does she respond to the seed you're imparting into her life?

Since you are not married, I am not referring to physical seed, but to your spoken words, to all that you are pouring into her life. Does she take it and receive it? Or does she ignore what you're depositing? Perhaps she doesn't ignore it, but doesn't seem to grasp it either.

Question #8: Does the oil flow and does it flow toward her?

The oil represents your gift, your anointing, your divine enablement. Whatever comes naturally to you in ability should flow out of you during the course of your relationship and it should flow towards her, meaning you should use your abilities to love her.

To really make my point, I'll use myself as an example. I am anointed to be creative, especially in the area of writing. I am also strong in the area of romance. I know what to do, when to do it, and how to do it. These abilities also extend to others, so that I can write or plan an event on behalf of another man, and it will have maximum impact. It will express exactly what he wanted to express, even without me asking him.

However, put me in a relationship with a woman I don't love with everything I am, and that flow is severely hampered. Many of my friends can tell how much I love a woman by that flow. Likewise, there are some gifts in your life that can be used to determine if you truly love her.

As you search for a wife, use these eight keys, or questions, to help you make the determination if a particular young lady is your wife.

The last two questions can best be explained by sharing with you a word I received from the Lord. It is both powerful and liberating. Matter of fact, it summarizes the entire eight keys:

'When looking for a wife, first find a wife whom you love with all your heart, because faith works by love. Second, make sure she sees who you are. This requires you to know who you are to accurately determine if she sees the real you. If she can not receive your spoken seed, she can not receive your physical seed. Understand, fertile ground does not resist the seed."

Does she see you?

Is she receiving you, recognizing those moments when you're in your lane? If not, her unbelief, or insensitivity, will hinder the flow of God in your life like it was hindered when Jesus tired to speak in His own city. God wants the rock to pour out rivers of oil. not block it. The only way she can help is to see who you are. Remember, ground that is prepared to receive your seed will see you in glory-form, not seed-form.

Recognize that just because you aren't perfect in a thing doesn't mean the answer doesn't flow through you. She should be able to recognize this, because what you are called to do will naturally flow out of you, whether you are developed in it or not. Remember, your call was given to you before you did any good or bad.

However, if you do not develop in character, and especially the character of that word, you won't see the fruit of that word in your life, and this could severely hamper your ministry, business, family, and call. You may definitely have the oil flowing out of you, but it's not benefiting you, because you won't develop in it and it will adversely affect your credibility and the quality of life you lead. This happened with Moses. His lack of development where his temper was concerned kept him from the promised land.

A woman who sees you will recognize this and begin to speak with you in the tone and texture according to what is going on with you and according to how you are wired, because she will be able to diagnose it and speak 'breathed-in' words. A woman who doesn't see you will chip away at the external things, trying to produce what she does see, thereby doing more damage to the vision, because she doesn't know what to fix.

When the oil begins to flow in your life, a woman who sees you – ground that was prepared to receive – will always encourage that flow and purposely draw out that flow to help you develop in it. A woman who doesn't see you will unwittingly dam up that flow, arguing with it, because she doesn't revere it.'

Loving Your Garden

Once you find the wife you're looking for, it will be your responsibility to love her as Christ loved the church (Gal 5:25). You are required to give yourself for her and to wash her with water by the word. She is your garden. Treat her as such, and take excellent care of her.

Be careful that you don't let the world's way of thinking influence how you approach your relationship with your wife, as their way of thinking will not get you the harvest you desire.

First, understand that you bear the greatest responsibility. In your marriage, you should be the initiator and sustainer. Whatever you desire in your marriage, you must give it and cultivate it. In all things, you take the lead, even if that means taking the lead in submitting, or getting under her mission. Lead others to support her and always be willing to give the best of yourself. If your wife puts in one hundred, you put in two hundred, because she is your garden. And God designed you to tend and keep her, while she was called to *help* you; not carry, or replace, you.

Second, Valentine's Day is something designed by women and jewelry stores just to get your money. Nevertheless, there is value in giving gifts of high cost. Such gestures are an indicator of where your heart is: "for where your treasure is, there your heart will be also" (mt 6:21). Also, women did not invent gold and diamonds, God did. And we are to imitate God as dear children (Eph 5:1).

As God promised to lavish us with gold, silver, and precious jewels (Is 54:11-12; Eze 16:11-12; Ps 45:9 & 13; 1 Kngs 10; Gen 2:11-12), so should we lavish upon our wives. God set the value, not women, and so such gifts are precious.

I am not saying that material possessions equate to love. Given out of the surplus of your huge bank account and devoid of your sincere emotions, they mean absolutely nothing. However, I am saying that material possessions and money can be used to express love. Gifts of great material value and huge financial cost mean a lot when they are given as an expression of extraordinary love. If those gifts are accompanied by your complete love, they will make a tremendous impact. That's why I believe you should do all you can to make the day you propose and your wedding day as special as possible. In my eyes, those days are seed sown for your life together. The memories you build from those two special days will serve as an anchor for your marriage when difficult days come. As much as you can deposit in the love bank when times are good, I suggest you do.

In some cultures, you were always required to pay to have the right to marry a young woman, and, what you paid was according to her perceived value. As an example, Rachel would have cost more than Leah, because she was more desirable. So, what is your perceived value of your wife and how desirable is she to you? I'm not suggesting that you go broke, but I am suggesting you stretch yourself beyond what is so comfortable it doesn't qualify as putting your heart into it.

Third, don't ever stop putting your treasure into your wife, not just money, but your time and actions. Always date your wife. Remember, faith works by love. So, energize her faith, as she seeks to bring increase into your life by bringing forth harvest of the seed you've sown into her. And since faith works by love, when you encounter challenges in life and need to see some things happen in your life, do two things.

1. Sow a sacrificial seed to God.

When you sow sacrificially to God, it moves Him, because He is aware that you've sown big because of the faith you have in Him. In the lives of Solomon and Cornelius, it was their gifts that persuaded God to show up.

> Now the king [Solomon] went to Gibeon to sacrifice there, for that was the great high place: Solomon offered a thousand burnt offerings on that altar. At Gibeon the Lord appeared to Solomon in a dream by night; and God said, "Ask! What shall I give you?"

1 Kngs 3:4-5

> A devout man and one feared God with his household, who gave alms generously to the people, and prayed to God always. About the ninth hour of the day he saw clearly in a vision an angel of god coming in and saying to him, "Cornelius!" And when he observed him, he was afraid and said, "What is it, Lord?" So he said to Him, "Your prayers and your alms have come up for a memorial before God."

> Acts 10: 2-4

2. Sow a sacrificial seed of love to your wife.

Your wife is your helper. Only two others – God and the Holy Spirit – are also called your helper. So, that puts her in rare company. If God, as a helper, is moved by your seed to him, then I believe your wife is also moved by great acts of love sown to her. Remember that the creative wisdom of God is working through your wife, as she is your garden. Sowing great acts of love, whether money, time, actions, or words, cultivates your garden so that it operates at its highest capability. And your garden functioning at its highest capability is what you'll need in the midst of challenges. Once again, faith works by love. Love your way out of difficult situations.

Loving your wife means coming before her in purity, sowing seeds of purity, not corruption. Be very mindful of the seeds you sow into your garden. Just like you wouldn't sow thorns and thistles into a physical garden, you shouldn't sow them into your wife. Why then would you go to strip clubs and watch pornography to arouse yourself and then bring that seed home to sow into your garden? Those things do not produce seeds of love, but seeds of lust, because it is not your wife you truly desire at that time. It is the woman you've been meditating on that you desire. Prov 5:19 says:

> As a loving deer and a graceful
> doe, let her breasts satisfy you at all times, and always
> be enraptured with her love.

Your wife is the only one who should enrapture you. How would you feel if your wife desired another man, but had sex with you since you were available? You'd feel horrible, because all it would be is sex, not love.

You do not bring those seeds home to plant into your garden, because they will pollute the ground and bring forth harvest. And, sooner or later, one of you will engage in perverted and illicit acts. There will be no one to blame but yourself for bringing those seeds home. That's why God wants you to enter the gates of the inner courts with only linen garments on. Linen garments represent that which is clean (Eze 44:17). Come before your wife clean for that time is sacred as she opens herself to receive from you.

I believe your journey, now, will be a successful one. May God truly bless your endeavors.

It is time for us to rise up as men and select wives who are called to our purpose, so that the will of God may be fulfilled here on the Earth.

As the proper family structure is reestablished in the body of Christ, great increase will be able to take place, and we will once again be able to establish the supremacy of the Kingdom of God here on the earth. It is a new season and a new day. God is doing marvelous things. Let's take our place and fulfill His word:

Now the Lord had said to us:
"Get out of your country
From your family,
And from your father's house,
To a land I will show you,
I will make you a great nation,
I will bless you,
And make your name great;
And you shall be a blessing.
I will bless those who bless you,
And I will curse those who curse you;
And in you all families of the earth
shall be blessed."

Where ?
In that land.

Prayer For Prudent Wife

Father, I come before you now, through and by the blood of Jesus, asking for your help. Help me find a wife who is called unto my purpose. The Bible says, 'a prudent wife is from the Lord'. So, there is no other way I can obtain one, except through You. I ask for a wife who is modeled after Prov 31:10-31: a wife who is virtuous; of noble character; a wife of valor in the sense of all forms of excellence. I ask for a wife who labors in the gospel, is full of good deeds and charitable works; a wife of good understanding and beautiful appearance.

Further, may my wife be able to win people over without saying a word, because her conduct is chaste – morally faultless, pure, undefiled, and without blemish. May she have the incorruptible beauty of a gentle and quiet spirit, a spirit that has power under perfect control.

Because of you, Father, I know I have a wife who is reverent, temperate, faithful in all things, discreet, a teacher of good things, gracious, honorable, and a homemaker. She stands by me praying always, loving me and committed to me.

Thank you for bringing me my wife in robes of many colors. Therefore, I greatly desire her beauty. I love her and I cherish her just as Christ does the church, giving myself for her. And just as she submits to me, I submit to her, because the wisdom of God flows through her. I thank you for her now, in Jesus' name. Amen.

Note: After you pray this prayer for the first time, believe it's done. Don't ask Him again, but now thank Him for answering your prayer.

Scripture references:

Prov 19:14	Acts 9:36	Tit 2:2-5
Ps 45:9 & 11-14	Prov 8	Prov 31:10-31
1 Sam 25:3	1 Tim 3:11	Song 2:16
Prov 11:16	Phi 4:3	2 Pet 3:1-4
1 Sam 1:26-28	Eph 5:22-23	Prov 12:4

www.ingramcontent.com/pod-product-compliance
Lightning Source LLC
LaVergne TN
LVHW051646080426
835511LV00016B/2515